# Middlesex
# MURDERS

## LINDA STRATMANN

*To John and Janice*

First published 2010

The History Press
The Mill, Brimscombe Port
Stroud, Gloucestershire, GL5 2QG
www.thehistorypress.co.uk

British Library Cataloguing in Publication Data.
A catalogue record for this book is available from the British Library.

ISBN 978 0 7524 5123 7

Typesetting and origination by The History Press
Printed in India by Replika Press Pvt. Ltd.
Manufacturing managed by Jellyfish Print Solutions Ltd

# CONTENTS

# AUTHOR'S NOTE

I would like to extend my grateful thanks to everyone who has assisted me with the research for this book. As always, the friendly staff at the British Library, Colindale Newspaper Library and the National Archives have been invaluable, and I was especially delighted to be granted permission to view files in the National Archives which had, until November 2009, been closed. My thanks and good wishes are due to Garry Nathan and everyone at Moorcroft House for the information and a tour of a fascinating estate. I was delighted that a great-niece of Daisy Holt (chapter 6) shared some family memories with me. These personal details are what brings the past back to life and excite me more than any dry document! I would also like to thank the parish officers of St Martin's Church, Ruislip, and everyone at The Stag, Enfield for their help. My husband's advice and support as well as his willingness to drive me to the scenes of old crimes and trudge through muddy woods and fields in search of the best pictures is appreciated more than I can say.

All photographs taken by the author are the copyright of Linda Stratmann.

# 1

# MURDER ON THE HEATH

## *Hounslow Heath, 1802*

In 1802 Hounslow Heath was a dangerous place, long known to be the haunt of highwaymen and footpads. This remnant of the ancient forest of Middlesex covered about 25 square miles, and although it was crossed by roads, it was regarded as somewhere to be avoided, or at least passed through as quickly as possible, preferably in a well-guarded coach.

At Feltham, not far from the road which linked Staines and Hounslow, was the country home of 35-year-old John Cole Steele, described as 'a young man of very amiable character'. The proprietor of the Lavender Water Warehouse, No. 15 Catherine Street, near the Strand, he had married Mary Ann Meyer in 1798. Steele owned a lavender plantation at Bedfont, not far from Feltham, which he visited regularly to give instructions to his manager, Henry Mandy.

On the afternoon of Friday, 5 November 1802, Steele left his London townhouse for Feltham. He was wearing a drab-coloured greatcoat, a shorter coat, breeches with stockings underneath, a striped waistcoat, half boots and a smart round hat. He did not state exactly when he would return, although there was an arrangement that he and his family would gather to celebrate his wife's birthday on Sunday. When Steele failed to return on Saturday it was assumed that he had been detained by business and was staying overnight at Feltham, and there was no immediate alarm, but when he was not back for the birthday party his family became concerned.

On the Monday morning a messenger was sent to Bedfont and returned with the worrying news that Steele had set out for home on Saturday evening, and, unable to obtain a carriage, had decided to walk across the heath. On Wednesday morning, Steele's brother-in-law, lavender-distiller Thomas Meyer, went to Feltham to make enquiries. Steele was not at his house, and Henry Mandy confirmed that his employer had left for home at about 7 p.m. on Saturday evening, since when nothing had been heard of him. Steele had not been in the habit of carrying large sums of money and Mandy said that his employer had then had about twenty-six or twenty-seven shillings on him.

*Highwaymen rob a stagecoach on Hounslow Heath, c. 1720.*

Meyer asked Mandy and another gentleman called Hughes to help him search the heath, going along the Feltham to London road, Meyer and Mandy on the right and Hughes on the left. At a clump of trees near a gravel pit, on the south side of the road, Mandy picked up an old hat cut in pieces, which he handed to Meyer, but it was not the one that Steele had worn, being very much older and resembling a soldier's hat. The gravel pit was about 10 or 15 yards from the road, and as the men drew near, they saw what they thought was a piece of clothing. Pulling aside the rushes that covered most of the material, Mandy found a drab-coloured greatcoat concealed under the water and pulled it out. He recognised it as the one Steele had been wearing when he last saw him, and noticed that it had a spot of blood on the right shoulder. The three searchers consulted about what to do next and Meyer and Mandy decided to go to the nearby Hounslow cavalry barracks in Beavers Lane and obtain the help of the officers and men to search for Steele. When they returned they found that a great many more people had arrived to join in the search.

It was Hughes who found the body; about 200 yards north of the road, lying in a ditch by a clump of trees, with the turf from the bank pulled across to partly conceal it. Steele lay on his back, the flap of his coat over his face, and a strap around his neck. He was not wearing his hat, stockings or boots. When the body was lifted out Hughes saw that the face was covered in blood and dirt, and there had been a violent blow on the back of the head. The strap had once had a buckle which was broken off, and one end had a knife run through it, and the other end drawn through so it was very tight. About 50 yards away Hughes found a pair of shoes. A large stick was also found. The hat, stick and shoes were handed to Isaac Clayton, the beadle of Hounslow, and they were eventually placed before police magistrate Sir Richard Ford at Bow Street.

The body was conveyed to The Ship public house at Hounslow and a surgeon, Mr Henry Frogley, was called. He found an extensive fracture on the front of the head with lacerations of the skin, and another lacerated injury on the back of the head, both of which he thought had been inflicted with a blunt instrument such as a stick. There had also been a heavy blow on the right arm. The strap was tight enough to cause suffocation, but it was his opinion that the head wounds were the immediate cause of death. The difficult task of telling Mrs Steele of her husband's death fell to her mother, but initially she was spared the worst details, being told that he had died of a fit. The inquest was held at The Ship and returned a verdict of wilful murder against some person or persons unknown.

Suspicion fell on a man and a woman who had been seen travelling together in Rutlandshire, the man of a very dirty appearance, in a shabby coat but wearing a good quality hat and carrying a stick, the woman in half-boots and stockings which could have been the ones taken from Steele's body. Letters were sent to justices in Rutland and Leicester, urging that the most strenuous efforts should be made to apprehend the couple, but they were never found. Steele's family

*Hounslow Heath.*

placed an advertisement in a newspaper offering a reward of £50 for information leading to the capture of the murderers. Several known criminals were arrested on suspicion, but after questioning they were released. Four years went by and all hope of finding the guilty persons was gone.

On 17 September 1806, 26-year-old Benjamin Hanfield (who was then calling himself Endfield) was found guilty at the Old Bailey of stealing a pair of shoes, and was sentenced to transportation for seven years. While in Newgate Prison awaiting transfer to a convict ship, he found himself discussing robberies with the other prisoners, and when the murder of Steele was mentioned he let slip that only three men in England knew the truth of it. The rumour went around the prison that he was involved and was about to betray his associates, and this came to the attention of the authorities.

Hanfield was transferred from Newgate to a prison hulk in Langstone Harbour and shortly afterwards made his first official disclosure regarding Steele's murder to Sir John Carter, Mayor of Portsmouth. Hanfield said that he had once been a hackney-coachman and had enlisted in the military on at least five occasions, but admitted that he generally made his living by thieving, and had often been tried and convicted at the Old Bailey. According to the *Newgate Calendar* and a report in *The Times*, he had been taken dangerously ill and raved about the murder, saying he wanted to tell what he knew before he died. Hanfield's own account makes no mention of any illness. The official view of Hanfield's revelations was that he might well know something about the murder of Steele, but he could also have been hoping for a financial reward, or a reduction of his sentence, and it was vital to test the truth of his account, especially as he was incriminating others in his confession.

*The interior of Newgate Gaol.*

John Vickery, an officer of Worship Street police office, was sent to Portsmouth on 15 November, and brought Hanfield up to town in a coach. On the way the coach passed across Hounslow Heath and as it did so they passed by a clump of trees between the 10 and 11-mile stones, near where Steele had been murdered. Without any prompting, Hanfield pointed out the spot.

At Worship Street Hanfield told the magistrates that the murder had been committed by John Holloway and Owen Haggerty. He had known Holloway for six or seven years and Haggerty for seven or eight and had spent a good deal of time in the company of both, usually in public houses; the Turk's Head and Black Horse in Dyott Street, and the Black Dog in Belton Street. Holloway had no trade as far as he knew and had worked as a labourer. Haggerty, he thought, had been a bricklayer's or plasterer's labourer.

Hanfield was shown the broken hat that had been found on the heath and said it was very like the one Holloway had been wearing on the night of the murder.

According to Hanfield, he had been in the Turk's Head at the beginning of November 1802 when Holloway had asked 'if I had any objection to being in a good thing.' When Hanfield said he was willing Holloway had revealed it was to be a 'low toby' or footpad robbery, the details of which he would reveal in a day or two. Two days later, Holloway told him the robbery would be carried out on the following Saturday and they were to meet together with Owen Haggerty at the Black Horse. At that meeting Haggerty confirmed that they would be robbing a gentleman on Hounslow Heath who was known to carry property on him. How they knew this, Hanfield didn't know, only that Holloway had somehow found it out. Neither did Hanfield say how they knew that Steele would be on the heath that Saturday, since, according to Thomas Mandy, Steele did not have a regular day of the week for going to the plantation. The three walked to Hounslow, with a couple of stops at public houses on the way, the last one being The Bell at Hounslow. They arrived on the Heath at four, then proceeded until they came to the 11-mile stone. Holloway was carrying a large blackthorn stick.

It was almost dark when they reached a clump of trees and there they waited until the moon rose. There was light enough to see a man, who Hanfield later knew to be John Cole Steele, wearing a light-coloured greatcoat and walking alone in the direction of Hounslow. Hanfield accosted Steele, demanding money, and Steele, asking the footpads not to hurt him, gave something to Haggerty. Holloway asked if the victim had delivered his 'book' (a pocket-book or wallet used to carry money), but Steele said he did not have a book. Holloway insisted he must have a book, but when Steele again said that he did not Holloway came up behind him and knocked him down with his stick.

Hanfield took hold of the legs of the fallen man, who was begging 'do not ill-use me', while Holloway stood over him and Haggerty searched his pockets. The victim began to struggle. He was unexpectedly strong and put up a good resistance, crying out all the time, but just then the men heard the sound of an approaching carriage. Holloway said, 'I will silence the bugger' and delivered several blows to their victim's head and body. Steele gave a loud groan, and then a little afterwards another, after which he appeared to be dead. Hanfield, who was on his knees holding the man's legs, became suddenly alarmed for his own safety. He got up and said, 'John, you have killed the man,' to which Holloway retorted that he was lying as the victim was only stunned. At this Hanfield said he would leave, and did so, walking back towards Hounslow, while Holloway and Haggerty remained with the body.

Despite his eagerness to get away from the scene of the crime, Hanfield waited for his companions outside The Bell, and about an hour later the two appeared looking out of breath. Holloway was carrying a hat, a rather better quality one than the one he had been wearing, which had looked like a solder's hat and which he said he had destroyed and left behind. The three arrived at the Black Horse after midnight, finding the house shut for business but the landlord not yet in bed. They were able to obtain a drink, and shared half a pint of gin before parting for the night.

When they saw each other the next day Holloway was wearing the stolen hat, which was a little too small for him. On the following Monday he still wore the hat, which worried Hanfield as he thought it might lead to them being discovered. Looking into the hat he saw that the name of Steele was marked inside it, and pointed this out to Holloway, who promised to get the lining taken out. Holloway later told Hanfield that he had tied the hat in a handkerchief weighted it with stones and thrown it off Westminster Bridge.

After telling his story, Hanfield was taken to the heath by Vickery together with Mr Hughes and Isaac Clayton. Alighting from the coach at The Bell, Hanfield was told to walk where and how far he wished. Approaching the 11-mile stone, he pointed to the clump of trees where the body had been found.

Holloway, a stoutly built man, was arrested by Joseph Dunn, the parish officer of Paddington, and taken to Clerkenwell Prison. On the following day Vickery and an officer of Worship Street, Daniel Bishop, took him to court, after first reading to him the warrant charging him on suspicion of the murder of Mr Steele. 'Oh, dear!' exclaimed Holloway, 'I know nothing about it, I will down on my knees to you and the justice, if you will let me go.'

On 29 November Vickery arrested Haggerty, who was then aboard a frigate moored off Deal. Haggerty, who was slightly built, was too ill to be told the reason for his arrest. He was let down out of the ship into a boat, assisted by the nervous Vickery, who was unsure that the man would live long enough to reach London. That same morning Haggerty, whose voice was so faint he could hardly be heard, was questioned by the port admiral. Haggerty said that he had been a marine for two years, but could not remember where he had been three years ago. Asked about his movements four years ago, he failed to answer and almost fell. Vickery had to catch him, and he was allowed to sit and was given some water. Haggerty was too ill to travel and had to be left behind at Deal Hospital.

On 8 December Holloway and Haggerty appeared at Worship Street and were questioned by the magistrate, John Nares. Hanfield's statement was read to the two prisoners, who were questioned separately. Both men said they did not know each other, and were entirely innocent of the murder.

*The murder of John Cole Steele from the* Newgate Calendar.

Holloway, who was generally known under the name of Oliver, said that Hanfield was 'an entire stranger' and pointed out that in the statement made against him Hanfield had given the wrong name. He knew nothing of Hanfield, having only seen him in the street. He denied ever having been in Hounslow and said that in November 1802 he had been working for a Mr Rhodes and a Mr Stedman. Haggerty, who said that he knew no more of the offence 'than a child unborn', accused Hanfield of confessing only to get his freedom, and pointed out some minor contradictions in the accounts he had given at different times. He said he was never in Hounslow in his life, and in the winter of that year was working for a Mr Smith of Seven Dials.

The magistrate questioned the men whom the suspects said had employed them, but all denied that the accused had worked for them in 1802, although they had done so in other years. Some effort was made to show that Mr Steele's hat or boots might have fitted the prisoners but this was inconclusive.

Holloway and Haggerty were questioned seven times in all, and between these sessions they were confined in separate cells, with a partition sufficiently thin that they were able to converse with each other. Unknown to either, Officer Daniel Bishop was placed in a nearby privy from where he was able to overhear what they said.

The trial of John Holloway aged thirty-nine and Owen Haggerty, twenty-four, took place at the Old Bailey on 18 February 1807. The chief witness for the prosecution was Benjamin Hanfield, who had earned his immunity from prosecution. Before he gave evidence a portion of His Majesty's pardon was read out in court.

The defence took the line that Hanfield had only confessed for personal gain, and suggested that when in gaol Hanfield had boasted that he knew a way of getting his liberty and putting £500 in his pocket. Hanfield replied that the only mention he had made of £500 was to Mr Shuter the head turnkey when he had said that he was due the sum from a legacy but would not be able to get it. He insisted that his only motive in telling what he knew was 'compunction of conscience'. He said that no promises had been made to him to induce him to make his statement, and denied that he had ever informed against anyone for reward. Shuter later testified that he had never discussed the crime with Hanfield.

Hanfield, saying that he thought the murder was a cruel thing which had greatly troubled his conscience, admitted that despite this he had said nothing about it and had made no written note of what had happened during the four years that had elapsed since the crime. He had heard about Steele's family offering a reward of £50 but had not made any disclosure then. Despite the obvious suspicions about his motives, the impression made upon the court was that Hanfield knew a great deal about the murder.

Hanfield's story about the passing coach was supported by coachman John Smith, who testified that he drove the Gosport coach which left London at 6 p.m., arriving at Hounslow two hours later. The coach had left Hounslow on 6 November and was between the clump of trees and the 11-mile stone when he heard the sound of a man moaning in distress. The sound came from the north side of the road. He heard the groaning again, fainter than at first. Smith remarked to the passengers that he thought something was amiss, but he didn't stop.

Mr Gleed, for the defence, then observed that it was unnecessary to call any more witnesses to prove that Mr Steele had been murdered at that spot. 'There is no doubt that the witness, Hanfield, had a hand in the murder;' he said. 'The question is whether the prisoners at the bar had and whether they were the perpetrators of it or not ...'

Joseph Townsend, a Bow Street officer, was able to produce the original items of evidence; the shoes, the hat and the stick, which he described as a bludgeon, and the strap.

Although Holloway and Haggerty had claimed as part of their defence not to know each other or Hanfield, there were many witnesses who had known all three men for a number of years. There was clear evidence that the two prisoners knew each other, but their connection with Hanfield was less obvious, and many of the sightings were several years old. William Blackman testified that the two accused had been in each other's company often for the last four or five years, and four years ago he had seen all three together, yet he also said that he had only known Holloway for a year and a half. Edward Crocker, a Bow Street officer, said he had often seen Holloway and Haggerty in public houses in Dyott Street, and that Haggerty owned a blackthorn stick.

Christopher Jones, another Bow Street officer, said he had seen Haggerty and Hanfield together in different public houses and in the streets about three years ago. Collin M'Daniel, the publican of the Black Horse, said he had seen Hanfield and Haggerty travelling together, but this was about 'three or four or five years ago'. William Beale of the Turk's Head knew all three men and although he had never seen them all in company, Haggerty and Hanfield had both been at his house at the same time, though not drinking together. John Peterson, a porter, had often seen Haggerty and Hanfield at the Turk's Head, where he had served them with beer. What was unclear from much of the evidence was whether Hanfield and the accused had actually been in each other's company or whether they had simply been customers in the same public houses or in the street at the same time.

John Sawyer had lived at The Bell, Hounslow in 1802, but could only say he thought he had seen Holloway at Hounslow.

Officer Daniel Bishop now supplied the court with some extraordinary testimony. He claimed to have written down verbatim all the conversation that took place between Holloway and Haggerty which he had overheard from the privy, and read it out. It was obvious from his evidence that the two men knew each other well and were friends and had both lied when they had claimed not to know each other. In these reported conversations the prisoners had said that Hanfield was a lying villain and both were convinced that his evidence would not be accepted. Up to the time they were committed for trial they had felt that the most likely outcome was that their accuser and not they would suffer for the crime. Nothing in their conversation suggested that they had any complicity in or knowledge of the crime.

At the close of the trial it was apparent that Hanfield's evidence had been accepted as true, and the prisoners' failure to provide an alibi, as well as the lies they had told, had counted against them. Both were found guilty. When questioned further in prison they continued to assert their innocence. Hanfield disappeared. His subsequent career is unknown.

The execution of Holloway and Haggerty took place outside Debtors' Door of Newgate Prison on Monday 23 February, together with that of Elizabeth Godfrey for the murder of Richard Prince, whom she had stabbed in a quarrel.

The crowds that assembled were unparalleled and estimated at about 40,000 people. By 8 a.m. there was not an inch of ground around the scaffold unoccupied. Even before the prisoners arrived the crush was so great that people trapped in the crowd were crying out to be allowed to escape. When Holloway was brought out and pinioned he fell to his knees and protested his innocence. Rising, he proclaimed that both he and Haggerty were innocent of the crime. The frailer Haggerty declared the same. When Holloway ascended the platform, 'seemingly with an undaunted spirit', he bowed first to the left then to the right and addressed the multitudes: 'Innocent! Innocent, Gentlemen! No verdict! Innocent, by God!' Even after the cap was placed over his head he continued to repeat the word 'Innocent'. As the fatal moment approached the crowds surged with excitement.

At the corner of Green Arbour Lane, nearly opposite the Debtors' Door, two piemen were selling their wares when one man's basket was knocked over. He was bending down to pick up his wares when the surging crowds tripped and fell over him. There was an immediate panic, in which people fought with each other to escape the crush. It was the weakest and the smallest in the crowd who suffered. Seven people died from suffocation alone, and others were trampled upon, their bodies mangled. A broker named John Etherington was there with his twelve-year-old son. The boy

*The condemned cell,
Newgate Gaol.*

was killed in the crush, and the man was at first thought to be dead and placed amongst the corpses, but he survived with serious injuries. A woman with an infant at her breast saved her baby by passing it to a man and begging him to save its life. Moments later she was knocked down and killed. The baby was thrown from person to person over the heads of the crowd and was eventually brought to safety.

As the drop of the platform was struck away the three condemned fell, and were left to strangle to death. Gradually the mobs dispersed, and the bodies, thirty in all, were taken up in carts, twenty-seven to Bartholomew's Hospital, two to St Sepulchre's Church and one to The Swan public house. Numerous others were injured, including fifteen men and two women who were so severely bruised that they were taken to hospital, one of whom died the following day. At the hospital, the bodies were washed and laid out in Elizabeth ward, awaiting identification by relatives.

*Dead Man's Walk,
Newgate Gaol.*

The trial left behind considerable unease, and real doubts as to whether the evidence of Hanfield could be relied upon. Attorney James Harmer had been asked by the fathers of the accused to instruct counsel to defend them. At first he had been in no doubt as to their guilt, but as the trial had progressed he began to have misgivings. He spoke to Holloway and Haggerty many times after the trial and became convinced of their innocence. In 1807 he published a pamphlet making a number of points which suggested that Hanfield had lied. Harmer observed that at the trial Hanfield had said that he had seen Steele walking on the 'right side of the road going from London' i.e. the north side, the side on which the body had been found. Harmer made enquiries and discovered that Steele habitually walked on the south side of the road. He theorised that Steele had been attacked on the south side and had run from his attackers in the direction of the barracks on the north side hoping to get help.

*An execution at Debtors' Door, Newgate Gaol.*

Harmer spoke to the landlord of The Bell and his wife, who did not recall any strangers being in their house on the night of the murder, and neither did the landlord of the Black Horse recall being woken at midnight that night. Hanfield had claimed to be a hackney-coach man, but Harmer found that he had actually been a guard on the stagecoach on the Hounslow Road and also a soldier at Hounslow barracks, and was well acquainted with the area. The facts of the murder – where it had occurred and what articles were found nearby – were well-known through local gossip. Hanfield's evidence about Holloway wearing Steele's hat was not borne out by anyone else. Harmer also observed that as Steele had no routine there was no way that the men could have known of his journey that night. The stick found on the heath was not blackthorn, as described by Hanfield, but birch. When Harmer examined Hanfield's evidence carefully he realised that it lacked small detail. For the period immediately after the murder Hanfield had nothing at all to say, claiming that he had left the scene. Harmer was sure that this was to conceal the fact that he actually knew nothing about the crime apart from common gossip, because he had not been there.

Most damningly, Harmer found that Hanfield had tried the confession trick before. In 1805 he had been charged with desertion from the 9th Light Dragoons and had calculated that by confessing to a robbery he would avoid being returned to his regiment to be punished for desertion. When he confessed before the Bow Street magistrates, however, it was so obvious that he knew nothing of the burglary that he was acquitted and was later confined to military prison.

*The title page of the pamphlet by James Harmer.*

## Murder of Mr. Steele.

### DOCUMENTS

AND

### OBSERVATIONS,

TENDING TO SHEW

*A PROBABILITY OF THE INNOCENCE*

OF

### JOHN HOLLOWAY

AND

### OWEN HAGGERTY,

*Who were Executed on Monday the 23d of Febuary, 1807, as the Murderers of the above Gentleman.*

### BY JAMES HARMER,

ATTORNEY AT LAW.

### LONDON:

PRINTED FOR THE AUTHOR; AND SOLD BY M. JONES, 1, PATERNOSTER-ROW; AND MAY BE HAD OF ALL BOOK-SELLERS IN TOWN OR COUNTRY.

### 1807.

*Lewis and Hamblin, Printers, Paternoster-row.*

---

JOHN HOLLOWAY, &c.          373

cart-load of shoes, hats, petticoats, and other articles of wearing apparel, picked up. Until four o'clock in the afternoon, most of the surrounding houses had some person in a wounded state: they were afterwards taken away by their friends on shutters, or in hackney-coaches. The doors of St. Bartholomew's Hospital were closed against the populace. After the bodies of the dead were stripped and washed, they were ranged round a ward on the first floor, on the women's side: they were placed on the floor with sheets over them, and their clothes put as pillows under their heads: their faces were uncovered: there was a rail along the centre of the room: the persons who were admitted to see the shocking spectacle went up on one side, and returned out on the other. Until two o'clock, the entrances to the Hospital were beset with mothers weeping for sons! wives for their husbands! and sisters for their brothers! various individuals for their relatives and friends!

Seldom has such a scene of distress and misery presented itself in this metropolis.——When the gates were opened, a great concourse was admitted; and when the yard was full, the gates were again closed, until the first visitors retired from this scene of woe: as soon as any of the deceased were recognized, the body was either put into a shell, or the face covered over, with the name of the party written on a paper, and pinned over the body.

The next day (Tuesday) a coroner's inquest sat in St. Bartholomew's Hospital, and other places where the bodies were, on the remains of the sufferers. Several witnesses were examined with respect to the circumstances of the accident, which examination continued till Friday, when the verdict was, " That the several persons came by their death from compression and suffocation."

*An extract from the* Newgate Calendar *describing the aftermath of the tragedy following the execution.*

In September 1820 John Ward, alias Simon Winter, was indicted for the murder of John Cole Steele, committed in company with another man called Luke who was not in custody. Ward had lived in the neighbourhood of Hounslow, and a witness, R. Newton, had seen him close to the murder site on the Friday before the murder and on the Wednesday afterwards. The prosecution stated that a witness would tell the jury that the accused had demanded £20 from him. On his replying that he did not have 20 farthings, the prisoner had said, 'How would you like to have this round your neck?' showing him a strap very like the one he had later seen round the neck of Steele. A witness would testify that he had seen Newton and Ward on the heath on the Saturday, and another would state that on the Wednesday the prisoner had joined with him in the search for Steele's body. Shortly before the body was found Ward had gone in another direction, as if he knew where the body was and wished to lead him away from it. Ward had absconded soon afterwards and had not been seen in the neighbourhood again until a few days ago, when he had been recognised in a public house. Ward was already suspected of cow stealing and there was a £100 reward for his apprehension.

Mr Justice Heath was not convinced there was enough to go before a jury on Steele's murder as the case amounted to no more than bare suspicion. After looking at the depositions, the justices and recorder decided that there was insufficient evidence and directed that the prisoner should be acquitted. The mere fact that this case had been brought was, however, a public admission that the conviction of Holloway and Haggerty was no longer thought to be safe.

The fate of Holloway and Haggerty was often referred to in subsequent trials as an example of how little weight could be given to the evidence of accomplices to a crime. The tragedy which had attended their execution also gave rise to considerable anxiety for many years. In 1812, when John Bellingham, the assassin of Prime Minister Spencer Perceval, was executed, the events of 1807 were fresh in the public memory and the crowds were a great deal less than anticipated. In 1816 John Etherington, the man who had survived the crush, was tried for stabbing a rates collector with a sword. It was said that he had not been in his right mind since the tragedy. He was acquitted. As late as 1837 a warning letter was sent to *The Times* about the dangers of 'a large concourse of idle persons' coming to witness an execution.

Little remains of the old Hounslow Heath, most of which now lies beneath the runways of London Airport.

# 2

# THE BEADLE OF ENFIELD

## *Enfield Chase, 1816*

In 1816 John Draper was one of the beadles for the Court of Requests in Enfield. These minor courts were established in the reign of Henry VIII to deal with small debts, and Draper was responsible for collecting the sums judged to be due.

On the morning of Thursday 8 August Draper asked a friend, Richard Thomas, a schoolmaster of Barnet, if he would go with him to execute some orders of the Court of Requests, and point out the defendants to him. They set out at midday, travelling by horse-drawn cart, and accompanied by Draper's small bulldog. The first person they called upon was Daniel Chappel, who was arrested and taken to the sign of the Robin Hood and Little John at Potters Bar to settle his debt and costs, which totalled £2 18s 9d. Chappel sent for his attorney, Mr Reynolds, who came and paid the debt for him, handing over three £1 notes for which change was required. Draper pulled out a little red pocket-book bound about with string, which contained a thick roll of banknotes to which he added the three notes. Reynolds remarked at the amount of money the beadle was carrying and said he was surprised that Draper was not afraid to have such a quantity about him. Draper, unconcerned, said he always did so and put the book away in his breeches' pocket. A bulky, powerfully built man in his fifties, Draper regarded himself as a match for any man. By then it was about four o'clock, and the beadle must have considered his day's work done, for he and Thomas then drove on to the White Bear at Barnet for a drink. Thomas left at about ten minutes past seven, at which time Draper had consumed about two shillings' worth of drink, and was merry but not actually drunk.

Draper soon struck up an acquaintance with James Smith, a hairdresser, and the two men drank together. Smith had never met Draper before that day and was unprepared for the effect of alcohol on his companion who, during the course of the evening, became quarrelsome, boastful, careless and aggressive. After an altercation with the landlord, presumably about payment, Draper pulled out the small red pocket-book, saying, 'Here is enough to buy you all!' He did not open the book, but it must have been apparent to any observer that it was stuffed with banknotes. Smith needed to get home to Cheshunt and Draper offered to give him a lift in his cart. Half an hour later they left together, pausing on the way at another public house for more beer. They travelled on another 2 miles to Enfield and arrived at the Bald-Faced Stag on Enfield Chase between eight and half past, where they drank three glasses of gin and water, two of which Smith paid for.

James Tuck, the landlord, was an enthusiast of the sport of pugilism, or bare-knuckle fighting, and that night a group of pugilists in training were staying at The Stag, one of whom was African-American Samuel Robinson. Robinson, born in New York in 1778, had come to England at the age of 20. Tall and muscular, he was greatly in demand as a sparring partner and in 1816 was taking part in some of the most important contests of his career. A fighter of courage and tenacity, he was also noted for his sporting generosity towards his opponents. Outside the ring he was 'good-natured, rather humorous ... he has nothing like ferocity attached to his composition; and in society he is not inattentive to the rules of decorum.' Robinson had been lodging at The Stag for three weeks, together with two other fighters, Peter Saunders and Joseph Church, about whose characters nothing is known.

In the bar, Draper singled out Robinson and accosted him, trying to goad the pugilist into fighting with him. Smith thought Draper's behaviour 'rather insulting'. Taking out the same pocket-book he had displayed at Barnet, Draper offered to bet £10 or £20 on the outcome of the fight. Robinson very prudently said that he did

*A pugilist, c. 1816.*

not want to fight, and refused to strike Draper, but in view of the beadle's aggressive manner, added that if Draper struck him, he would apply to a magistrate and get the law on him. Draper put the red book away, but every man in the room would have been in no doubt that it contained a substantial sum of money.

Thwarted of his boxing match, Draper decided that he wanted his dog to fight James Tuck's dog. He went out and returned carrying his dog, took off its chain and collar, threw it down, and urged it to fight. Tuck refused to allow this, and secured his own dog. Draper was by now so obviously drunk and his behaviour dangerously out of control that several people tried to get him to leave, and Tuck repeatedly told him to go. Smith, who was anxious to get home, also tried to persuade Draper to leave, but the beadle was far from done with his evening's drinking. By ten o'clock Smith gave up on the promised lift, wished Draper goodnight and set off on foot. He had walked for about twenty minutes when Draper's horse and cart, which had been left in the inn yard, came up behind him, and he saw that there was no

*The side exit of The Bald-Faced Stag (nowadays The Stag), leading to Gentleman's Row.*

*Gentleman's Row near the Bald-Faced Stag, with houses dating back to the sixteenth century.*

driver. Smith decided he couldn't leave Draper at the public house without any means of getting home, so he got into the cart and drove it back to the pub. There he found Draper in the same company as before and again urged him to go. Draper said he would when he had had another glass or two. Rather unwillingly, Smith stayed on for another hour. '[Draper] was then quite drunk,' said Smith later, 'he was stupidly drunk.'

Noticing that the horse had once again moved the cart away from the door, Smith and Draper both went to find it, and as they crossed the field immediately outside the pub, they met The Stag's ostler, William Roberts. Draper got hold of the man by the collar and demanded to know where his horse and cart were. The ostler said he knew nothing about them, upon which Draper shook him angrily. There was a struggle and both men fell to the ground. Draper got up, and next confronted a haymaker called William Webb, who had paused outside The Stag with his team of horses and some fellow workers to enjoy a pot of porter. Webb was just about to go home when Draper seized him by the collar and said he would wrestle with him. 'My friend,' said Webb, 'I am no wrestler.' Draper kicked Webb twice on the shins, and Webb tripped him, but the beadle clung on and both men fell to the ground. They struggled up, Webb, with an injured elbow, unable to detach himself from the drunken man, but when Webb tripped him a second time, Draper let go. 'My friend, I shall not hurt you,' said Webb and helped Draper up. The beadle came at him again and this time, Webb gave Draper an impatient shove and the man fell back, landing on his rear. Smith and Mrs Tuck, the landlord's wife, intervened while Webb made his departure. Draper was brought into the parlour, where there were a number of others present: Samuel Robinson; Walpole, a butcher; Holmes, a constable; Peak, a blacksmith; and landlord James Tuck, as well as lodgers Richard Crouch and Peter Saunders and several others. Draper and Smith were served with another drink. Smith again tried to get Draper to leave, without success, and unable to obtain any lodging he set out for home, alone and on foot.

John Walpole was a neighbour of Draper's and successfully persuaded the beadle that it was time to go. Draper went out to look for his horse and cart and Tuck asked Roberts the ostler to go out and check on him, but all he found was Draper's little bulldog tied up in the yard.

James Smith was within half a mile of Enfield when he again encountered Draper's driverless horse and cart. He didn't know where Draper lived, but guessed that if he got on the cart and gave the horse its head it would find its way home. The horse eventually stopped outside a house, and when Smith knocked on the door it was answered by Mrs Draper. Smith told her he had left her husband at the Bald-Faced Stag and she said she hoped he would get lodging there as it was so late.

Shortly before midnight Charles Johnson, a carman employed by Squire Paris of Beech Hill about a quarter of a mile away, was driving past the Bald-Faced Stag. By the light of the moon he saw James Tuck, the landlord, coming out of the front door in the company of three other men whom he did not know. They went round the corner towards the yard, and Tuck said, 'Damn his old eyes, he's gone this way, I know he is gone round here.' One of the other men said, 'Damn him, we will kick him and give him a good hiding.' Johnson continued his journey and heard nothing further of the events at the pub, but he knew Tuck well and recognised his voice.

At seven the following morning, Mary Holborn, the maidservant of the Bald-Faced Stag, took a pail and went to draw water from a well which lay in a field about 20 or 30 yards to the rear of the premises. The well, which was full almost to the top with water, was about 7 yards from the footpath, and the ground was banked up around it to a height of about 8 or 9 inches. Some 6–8ft across, it was only partly railed around, and two logs were laid over it crosswise leaving enough space for the pail to be let down, the rest of the space being covered with bushes and fern. The rail was not very robust, the wood having partly rotted away, and the maidservant noticed that part of it had been broken since she was last there. As Mary dipped the pail, she saw a hat in the well which appeared to be sitting on the water, and then she realised that it was on top of a man's head. Alarmed, she ran for Tuck, who was letting the fowls out of the fowl-house, and told him that there was a man in the well. Tuck went and looked. 'Good gracious!' he said, 'I suppose it is the poor old hostler [*sic*]'. Robinson was outside cleaning his shoes, when Tuck told him about the body in the well and asked him to call Crouch and Saunders, who came downstairs at once. All four men went to the well where they saw the body in an upright position, only the head being visible. It was John Draper. The body was lifted out of the well

*Behind the Bald-Faced Stag, probable site of the well in which John Draper was found, 2009.*

and laid on the bank for about a quarter of an hour to allow the water to drain from the sodden clothing, and then it was placed on a board and taken to the brew house. Tuck locked the brew house door, pocketed the key, and sent a boy on horseback to Enfield to tell Draper's relatives of his death. Tuck appeared visibly shocked by the discovery and was unable to eat his breakfast.

Draper's brother, a tinplate worker called David, arrived at The Stag at 9 a.m. together with Draper's son, who was also called David. (They may well have been the two David Drapers recorded in the 1841 census of Enfield, in which case Draper senior was about 50 in 1816, and his nephew 25.) Tuck told the two men that Draper had had a scuffle with the ostler, wrestled with a haymaker and had been found in the well. He accompanied them to the brew house and unlocked the door. David Draper senior, knowing that John was in the habit of carrying large sums of money, asked Tuck if he had taken charge of his brother's property. Tuck said that whatever property the dead man had about him he had then, and he knew nothing of any property. At the sight of the body, Tuck became very agitated. He looked nauseous and turned away, retching, going to the other end of the brew house. The Drapers searched the dead man's pockets but found only two large letter cases which held court papers, and a purse containing nine shillings and a halfpenny. Of the small red pocket-book and its roll of banknotes there was no sign.

Mr Clarke, a surgeon of Enfield, made a brief examination of the body on 10 August. Having been informed by Tuck that the man had been fighting before his death, he was not therefore surprised to find bruises around the face and neck which appeared to have been made by a fist. Since the body had been found in a well, he thought that was sufficient cause of death.

The inquest was held at the Bald-Faced Stag, and excited considerable public interest, the inn yard being thronged with people all day. The jury first inspected the body and then the well. Tuck told the coroner that Draper had left the pub at about half past ten. At midnight, being told that Draper's dog was still in the yard, he went out to search for him thinking he might have fallen asleep. The only other person with him was Richard Crouch. He denied using the words attributed to him by Johnson. Crouch, who had lodged at the pub for a fortnight, said he had seen Draper there on the Friday, but he had not heard any betting going on, nor seen Draper produce any money. At midnight he had gone to the door with Tuck but no further and denied either hearing or using the words reported by Johnson. He added that the two pugilists, Church and Robinson, had then already been in bed an hour.

Mr Unwin, the coroner, observed that although a great suspicion had arisen that Draper had been robbed and then killed to screen the robbery, 'yet, however just might be the grounds for the first of these imputations, the second was not so clear.' He pointed out that Draper had been excessively intoxicated, and, on his way to the yard where his cart had been left, would necessarily have passed near to the well,

*The Bald-Faced Stag (nowadays The Stag).*

and could have fallen into it by accident: '... there was a difficulty in conceiving that he could have been forced into this well, unless he had been first violently deprived of all sensation, in which case some external marks of injury would have been visible.' Considering the position and the dimensions of the well, he thought there were difficulties with either theory, but suggested that the jury would decide on the 'superior probability'. The jury obediently returned a verdict of accidental death.

After the inquest was over, the undertakers arrived to put the body in a coffin, supervised by the two David Drapers, who soon approached the coroner. They said that they had discovered blood on Draper's clothes, and a potentially fatal bruise under his left ear, and were convinced that he had been murdered. Unwin immediately ordered Clarke to re-examine the body and report the result to him. He told the relatives that if it should appear that any violence had been offered to the deceased he would proceed with a further investigation and call for the aid of police magistrates.

Clarke, together with a Mr Holt of Edmonton, carried out a second and more detailed post-mortem examination on 13 and 14 August and reported that they had found the mark of a violent blow under the left ear of the deceased which they believed was certainly enough to stun him, and might even be the cause of death. Clarke's excuse for missing it the first time was that the changes due to the warm weather had made it more visible. Both doctors were of the opinion that the wound was not caused by falling into the well. The jury demanded a new inquest, but as the first one had been conducted legally the original verdict had to stand, and could only be set aside by the Court of the King's Bench. The surgeon's report was placed before the Secretary of State, and on 19 August James Tuck was charged with the wilful murder of John Draper and brought before the magistrates at Hatton Garden Police Court. The office was crowded and the event had attracted so many people that the roads outside were almost impassable.

Mr Reynolds, the attorney, testified that he had paid Draper a debt on behalf of his client. He was handed a banknote, which was one of a parcel of notes that had been in Tuck's possession, and was asked if he had ever seen it before. 'The note now produced is one out of the three notes I paid Mr Draper,' said Reynolds. 'It was the outside note of a parcel, and was marked 191. I am sure it is one of the notes I paid him; I have no manner of doubt about it.'

Mr Phillip Etteridge, clerk to Mr Brailesford, an Enfield brewer, gave evidence that he had called at the Bald-Faced Stag at eleven o'clock on the morning of 8 August for payment. He spoke to Mrs Tuck, who said that he had called too early and she did not have the money ready for him. Etteridge had other calls to make so he went on and returned to The Stag at four that afternoon. He again saw Mrs Tuck and asked her if she would send him some money by eight o'clock the next morning. She told him he might depend on having it. At eleven o'clock the following morning, Benjamin Petts, the Tucks' errand boy, arrived at the brewery on horseback with the money and handed it to a lad named Charles Smith in the counting house. Charles endorsed his name on the back of each note and when Etteridge arrived the bundle was handed to him. In all there were eighteen £1 notes and £2 in silver.

Etteridge confirmed that the note which had been identified by Mr Reynolds as one he had paid to Draper on 8 August, was one of those eighteen notes.

Mrs Street, the wife of a labourer of Enfield, was also able to identify another of the notes used by Tuck to pay the brewer. On 30 July she had paid a debt to Draper, and it included a note which had some writing on the back which she particularly remembered. He had remarked that as it was a new note he would keep it by him. Mrs Street had described the writing on the back to David Draper senior before she was shown the note produced in court.

At this point in the proceedings the magistrate called in Mrs Tuck, but in keeping with the law of evidence he could not ask her any question whose answer might incriminate her husband. Mrs Tuck was asked where and from whom she received the notes she had sent to the brewers and whether she had received any notes from John Draper the night before he died. Mrs Tuck replied that she had about £10 in £1 notes and borrowed six more that night from Mr Peak in the back parlour. She then tied up the parcel and gave it to her husband to send off the next morning. It cannot have escaped the court that she had accounted for only sixteen of the eighteen notes.

Mrs Tuck withdrew and the prisoner was brought forward. He was described by *The Times* as 'a tall groom-like looking man; he had a black eye; his house is well known as a training house to the noted prize-fighters of the day', while the *Morning Post* stated that Tuck was tall and athletic, his features 'rather good than otherwise' adding, 'His hair is cut in the pugilistic fashion, and his whole appearance is that of a prize-fighter.'

The magistrate told Tuck that it had been proved that two of the notes paid by him to the brewer had been in the possession of the deceased, one of them, the note seen by Reynolds as late as 4 p.m. on the day before Draper's death. 'I now call on you to tell from whom you received them, as it is necessary for you.'

'I never take or change any notes,' said Tuck. 'I cannot tell where my wife took them.'

Benjamin Petts confirmed that his master had given him a parcel to deliver saying it contained money, but he had not seen how much was in it. One of the officers of the court produced more money in evidence, six £1 notes he had found on Mrs Tuck and two £40 and a £1 note found on Crouch and Saunders. Tuck was then remanded for further examination, also to give more time in case the rest of the notes could be identified by people who had paid money to the beadle.

Tuck was examined again on 22 August. The proceedings lasted five hours and attracted huge numbers of interested onlookers, so much so that tradesmen set up fruit and oyster stalls in the street, which began to resemble a fair.

At three o'clock on the afternoon of 8 August, Constable John Holmes had gone to The Stag to execute a warrant against the pugilist Church, at the suit of a Mr Hill. He recalled that Draper had arrived there between eight and nine, and was 'rather intoxicated'. Holmes had intended to accompany Draper home in his cart, but at about eleven o'clock, he had suddenly noticed that Draper was no longer in the parlour, and that Tuck, Crouch, Saunders and Robinson had also gone.

He had later seen Tuck at about midnight but did not see the others again that night. He assumed that Draper had 'given him the double', and went out into the street to enquire after him, but was not able to find where he had gone. Shortly afterwards he left the house. Holmes knew where the well was situated; behind The Stag and not on the way to Draper's house. He thought there must have been 'some foul play'.

James Peak, the blacksmith, confirmed that he had lent six £1 notes to Mrs Tuck, and she had said that this would just make up the amount she wanted. Mary Holborn told the court that in her opinion anyone stumbling across the well could not have fallen into it.

The magistrate addressed James Tuck, pointing out that Draper was at his house until eleven o'clock on 8 August with a pocket-book containing a large sum in banknotes and that the following morning two of those notes were included in a bundle used by Tuck to pay his brewers bill. It was also proved that Tuck and three others had gone out to search for some person who they had threatened. 'How do you account for this?' he asked.

Tuck replied that the last time he had seen Draper was at 11 p.m. and as the horse and cart had gone he had assumed that the man had followed. He had gone out later and called to the old ostler, who was deaf, to let the cow and calf out, and he had then noticed that Draper's dog was still in the yard. He was alarmed, thinking that perhaps Draper had not gone home but had lain down to sleep somewhere, and told the ostler to go and look for him. Crouch, Saunders and Robinson were with him at the time. The ostler returned saying he could not find Draper. Tuck said that he had then gone to bed. He was unable to account for the notes coming into his possession as Draper had paid him no money and he never gave change for notes. Tuck then supplied the broadest possible hint that the old ostler may have been involved. He had no character (i.e. references) for him; the man had simply come to him asking for a job, saying that he had lived for many years in the service of Lord Cowper from whom he had half a guinea a week pension. Tuck had employed the man because there was a great deal of company coming to The Stag at the time because of the pugilists in training. Tuck added that the ostler had since left as he had been detected in robbing his wife, and he thought he was living in Swallow Street.

The magistrate questioned the four pugilists. On 8 August Robinson had been hay making at Enfield during the day, in company with Walpole, Church, Crouch and Saunders, before returning to The Stag for the evening. After he had refused Draper's challenge the beadle was pulled away from him and 'grew quiet, finding no person took notice of him.' Robinson, saying that he 'could not sit unmolested', decided to go to bed at a quarter to ten, but Crouch and Saunders did not come up to the room for another hour and a half. Robinson said he had seen the Drapers search the pockets of the dead beadle, and contrary to the evidence given by them both, said he had seen Draper junior remove not only a black pocket-book, but a small red one, which was very full and tied round with string. Draper senior had said 'was that it?' and his nephew had said it was and put both items in his pockets. Robinson added that Saunders was also there and had asked the Drapers to open the pocket-books and examine the contents for fear anything should be missing and they might be blamed, but the Drapers had both objected to doing this, saying that everything was safe. Shown a red pocket-book in court Robinson said that was not the same as the one he had seen, which was smaller.

Saunders was a poor witness; he said he had been in and out of the parlour during the evening of 8 August had taken no notice of what went on and couldn't remember anything of importance. He had to be prompted to recall accompanying Tuck into the field to look for Draper. Saunders agreed with Robinson that he had been present when the Drapers had searched the body and removed two pocket-books. The £40 note found on him he had received the previous July. Crouch was able to add nothing more to the others' stories.

The magistrate remarked that all the evidence had now been gone through but it was necessary to locate the ostler, and as the case was 'intricate and mysterious' further enquiries would have to be made. Tuck was remanded again.

His final examination took place on 29 August when the magistrate addressed the large audience which had assembled, saying that he had received several anonymous letters, of which he could take no notice, but if any of the writers of these letters were present he would be prepared to meet with them in a private room to hear what they had to say. No one owned up to having written a letter and the prisoner was brought in.

Joseph Church, according to his fellow pugilists, had been 'so beat' (presumably in a recent bout) that he had thus far been unable to give evidence, but a deposition had been taken and was read out in court. He too claimed to know nothing of what had befallen Draper and described Robinson as '... a very quiet inoffensive man, and would not offer insult to any person ...'

Tuck was committed to be tried at the Old Bailey, and requested that instead of being transferred to Newgate to await trial he remain in the house of correction. 'I am an innocent man, and this will be the ruin of me,' he said. The judge granted the request and in view of the huge crowds that had gathered outside ordered the officers of the court to protect Tuck from any insult.

The trial opened on 20 September amidst considerable public interest and was presided over by Mr Baron Graham. The court was so crowded that several ladies were obliged to stand in the dock within 2 or 3ft of the prisoner and it was necessary to employ a posse of constables to clear a path through the crowds to enable the witnesses to enter.

Tuck appeared smartly dressed in a drab-coloured frock coat, buff waistcoat, white cord small clothes, and drab gaiters. Onlookers thought he resembled the MP William Huskisson. Despite his previous athletic appearance, he was now very lame, and was provided with a chair. Tuck was charged with having beaten Draper about the head and neck with his two hands, inflicting wounds which had occasioned his death and also with having thrown him into the well, causing death by suffocation and drowning. There was a second indictment charging him with the theft of the two £1 notes. He pleaded not guilty.

*Interior of the Sessions House, Old Bailey.*

None of the boxers were now claiming that the Drapers had taken the red pocket-book, which suggests that their testimony before the magistrates had not been truthful. Whether this meant they were involved in the murder, were covering up for Tuck, who was a friend, or were simply afraid that though innocent, they might be blamed, cannot be determined.

Richard Crouch said that Tuck always spoke to Draper kindly. As he saw the beadle drive up he said '... here is Mr Draper coming, as good an old man as ever lived.' Crouch added that Tuck had told him that he understood that Draper had once been a man of considerable property, but through some misconduct of his own or law affairs, his relations had got it. Tuck and Draper had shaken hands and '... there seemed to be a cordiality and friendship between them.'

Considerable efforts were made to challenge Johnson's evidence as to timing, however two fellow carters testified that all three had set off from Squire Paris', a quarter of a mile from The Stag, just before midnight. Johnson had driven on and the other two had gone indoors and asked for bread and cheese. Inside the bar they had seen no sign of Tuck or the pugilists. It was past hours, and the servant boy had been sent out of the back door to speak to Tuck and get his approval for serving food. One of the carters, Samuel Bricket, said that he did not see four men rush out of The Stag, or hear anyone make an exclamation or shout. As he had walked into the house Johnson had been going on his way. He thought that if anyone had rushed out he would have seen them and if they had said anything he would have heard them.

Johnson said that he was on good terms with Tuck, although on the previous Monday Mrs Tuck had refused to serve him beer after twelve o'clock, and when he persisted, one of the pugilists, Church, had come to the door and knocked him down the steps. Mr Reynolds testified about the banknote but was somewhat taken aback at being forced to admit that he had placed a bet on Tuck being convicted.

The defence then brought a great many witnesses as to the good character of the accused, declaring him to be honest and of a good temper, and a stranger to any feelings that might prompt him to commit robbery or murder.

Baron Graham summed up. There was no doubt in his mind that Draper had been murdered. The blow under the ear 'appeared to have been dealt by a person well skilled in the science of producing stupefaction at least, if not death, by one effectual stroke' while two witnesses had sworn that 'no blows had been struck during the trifling wrestling that had taken place'. In his opinion the most material evidence was that of Johnson and Reynolds, but the jury must also consider the probability of such a crime being committed by a man of good character. The jury deliberated for half an hour after which they presumably decided to give Tuck the benefit of the doubt, and found him not guilty. Tuck, who had been looking despondent, cheered up and bowed delightedly to the court. He was about to leave, when it was pointed out that he was still due to stand trial for robbery, and he was detained. On the following day he was tried for stealing the two £1 notes but the prosecution declined to offer any evidence and he was discharged. The murder of John Draper was never solved.

# 3

# MURDER IN MAD BESS WOOD

*Ruislip, 1837*

Ruislip woods, rich with hornbeam, oak, birch, alder and aspen, and home to many rare species of plants, covers over 730 acres and was designated a national nature reserve in 1997. It is not one wood, but four: Park Wood, Copse Wood, Bayhurst Wood and Mad Bess Wood. There are many explanations for the origins of the name Mad Bess Wood, one of which suggests it was so-called because Bess, the demented wife of an eighteenth-century gamekeeper, once roamed the wood looking for poachers. What cannot be disputed is that poaching and theft of timber was once a serious problem.

The north east section of Mad Bess Wood is known as Young Wood. It lies where Ducks Hill Road cuts between Mad Bess Wood and Copse Wood, about half a mile south of Ducks Hill Farm. In 1837 Ducks Hill Farm was occupied by Charles Churchill, a 28-year-old farmer, with a wife, Ann, and three small children. Churchill employed a number of labourers, one of whom was 15-year-old John Brill. The boy's father, James Brill, was a 49-year-old agricultural labourer and he and his wife Rachael and their six children lived in St Catherine's End, less than a mile from Young Wood.

In November 1836 John Brill, 'a good-tempered inoffensive boy', had given evidence before the Uxbridge magistrates against two men, Thomas Lavender and James Bray junior, who had been charged with poaching. Both men were convicted and threatened the boy with a violent revenge. By February the following year the two poachers were free and back in Ruislip.

On the morning of Thursday 16 February John left his home at a quarter past six to work on his master's farm. It was Uxbridge market day, and Churchill and his wife were due to go out at about 10 a.m., but before he left, Churchill gave John his orders for the day. The boy was to take three cows to the meadow, then, using a billhook and a stout glove, he was to cut bushes to fill up some gaps in the hedge.

*Ducks Hill Road, looking south from Ducks Hill Farm.*

*The entrance to Young Wood.*

This done, he should take the path leading from Churchill's house to Young Wood, and keep a watch over some poles which had been cut there, and also watch that the underwood (small trees and shrubs growing between the larger trees) should not be stolen. John was told to keep watch until 1 p.m. and then return to the farmhouse for his dinner. Churchill said that if anyone came to cut the wood, John was not to approach them, but let them cut as much as they wanted and take it away, just so long as he got near enough to see who it was. Churchill had had underwood cut and stolen from his property several times before and he was sure that the culprit would be someone he knew.

On the way to market Churchill called in at the Six Bells public house on Ruislip Common. A man called Medhurst came in and said, 'Churchill, did you hear a gun go off in your cover?' Churchill knew about the threats made against John Brill by Bray and Lavender and decided to go and check if all was well. It was then about 10.30 a.m. and he found the boy hard at work filling up the gaps in the hedge. Satisfied, Churchill continued on to market, returning at 3 p.m. He expected John to be at the gate to let him in, but the boy was not there. It is a measure of Churchill's concern that he at once went to search for the boy. This was not an easy task since the underwood, which covered the whole of Mad Bess Wood, was very thick and stood some 5ft high. Most of the paths through it were the blind paths of hare tracks. As *The Times* later commented, it was 'a place well adapted for the perpetration of any atrocious crime without the chance of immediate detection.'

Churchill did not find John Brill so he went to see the boy's parents, from whom he learned that John had not returned home. Churchill, James Brill and another man set out for the wood together and the search continued by the light of lanterns until almost ten o'clock that night. At first light the next morning the search was resumed, Churchill sending his men out in a number of directions, but they returned having found no sign of the missing boy. Throughout the Friday and Saturday volunteers trudged through Ruislip woods looking for John Brill. The weather had been dry but on Saturday night, and early Sunday, it rained.

On Sunday morning a large body of villagers joined in the search, including one of James Lavender's sons, and an associate of his, 35-year-old labourer Charles Lamb who lived near the Six Bells. James Lavender was the father of Thomas, who had been convicted on John Brill's evidence, and he and his family lived on Ruislip Common, about a third of a mile south of the wood. There were other Lavender, Bray and Brill households in the area, all of whom must have known each other. Thus far, James had not joined in the search, but that morning his wife Mary had said to him, 'Why don't you go and look after that poor boy, it looks so un-neighbourly.' James replied, 'Very well, I might as well go for an hour or so.' According to his own later evidence, as he went out of the house his parting words to his wife were, 'it would be a curious thing if after so many persons have been searching for him I should find him after all.' Less than a quarter of an hour after entering the wood James Lavender found John Brill, and called out 'Murder, here!' Churchill and his men came running.

The boy's body was in a hollow in a thick piece of high-standing wood. The earth where he lay was very soft and was covered in leaves and moss. He was lying on his back and was obviously dead. There was the mark of a severe blow under the right ear, which was very much swollen and which had bled profusely, and his front teeth had been knocked out. His clothes were in disarray and his face was covered in dirt as if he had been rolled in the decaying leaves that covered the spot. About 6 yards behind him his billhook and glove lay on the forest floor, but his cap was hanging high on a bush. Lavender lifted the body and put it over his shoulder. The head was unusually lax, as if the neck was broken, and blood dropped out of the nose and ear. The body and the ground around it were damp from the rain, but underneath the body the ground was dry. It might at first have seemed that John had fallen from a tree whose bough hung over the spot about 10ft from the ground, but once the body was removed Churchill examined the soft earth and could see no mark of an impression that would have been left by a fall. He also felt sure that the bough was not thick enough to bear the weight of the boy. He looked for signs of a scuffle, but saw none. The body was taken to the Six Bells about 500 yards from the entrance of the wood, where it remained for the inquest.

On the following Monday morning Churchill went into the wood again and saw that some underwood had been cut some 20 or 30 yards from the place where the body had been found. Suspicion had naturally fallen on the poachers who had threatened the boy's life and as a result of a message sent to Mr Thomas Dagnall, a

*The Six Bells public house. (By kind permission of the owner, Mark Cooper)*

*St Martin's Church, Ruislip, the probable burial place of John Brill.*

county magistrate who lived at Cowley, near Uxbridge, warrants were issued early that day for the arrest of Thomas Lavender, James Bray junior and their associate Charles Lamb. Murray, the police constable of Uxbridge, and other officers proceeded to Ruislip, took the men into custody and brought them before Thomas Dagnall and Sir William Saltonstall Wiseman Bt. at Uxbridge magistrates' court. The little town was soon crowded with people flooding in from the surrounding area, all anxious to hear the evidence. In view of the seriousness of the crime, Sergeant Charles Otway was sent from London to help the Uxbridge magistrates, an early example of the Metropolitan Police offering assistance with investigations outside London.

Lamb was brought in heavily shackled, his face ashen with fear: 'He exhibited symptoms of great depression of spirits'. The first witness examined was James Brill, who said that the hollow where his son's body had been found was close to a blind path used by hares, and also about three or four poles (a pole was 5½ yards) from a footpath.

Henry Meadows, the 61-year-old gamekeeper to local landowner Mr Dean, said that at seven o'clock on Sunday night a man came to his house urgently wanting to see him. The magistrates recommended that Meadows not name the visitor. Meadows said that he had not been at home at that hour, but shortly afterwards he met the man about 20 yards from his house, who said, 'I want to speak to you very particularly.' The man appeared to be very depressed and unhappy, and after a great deal of hesitation he suddenly turned round and said, 'Shall you be at home tomorrow morning?' Meadows said he would, and it was agreed that the man would speak to him then. On the Monday morning the visitor appeared, and said that he could bring proof that on the Thursday, the day on which it was assumed that John Brill had been murdered, Charles Lamb had twice been seen coming out of the wood. That man, Meadows promised, would be in court to give evidence on the following day.

Lamb told the court that he was innocent of the murder and was removed.

The next prisoner to appear was Thomas Lavender, a strongly built labourer of about 24. He also wore heavy handcuffs, but unlike Lamb, he did not appear to feel the seriousness of his situation. He stepped up to the bar boldly, and stated that he was innocent.

Meadows said that Lavender was one of the men against whom John Brill had given evidence and who had threatened that he would 'whip him up to a tree some day or other.' Meadows added that on the Sunday morning Lavender had been in the Six Bells, and on hearing it mentioned that Lamb had been seen going into the wood he had said that Lamb was 'a bloody fool for doing so as the boy's mother had said that he, Lamb and Bray had killed the deceased, and that if he could catch hold of her, he would kick her till the blood ran from her nose.'

The third prisoner, James Bray junior, a 25-year-old labourer, was brought handcuffed into the room, pale and white-lipped.

Rachel Brill, John's mother, was questioned. She denied ever having accused Lavender and his associates of the crime, and said that she had not until now suspected them of being involved. She had however heard that a lad named Henry Hill had called on her daughter Mary, and told her to tell 'Jack' to take care of himself, as 'Jem Bray' had said he would murder him when he had the opportunity.

Sir William said that '... there could be no doubt that a most atrocious murder had been committed, to discover the perpetrators of which it behoved every person to exert themselves to the utmost.' Since there was further evidence to be heard he remanded the prisoners. The three accused were then removed separately to the Uxbridge, Hillingdon and Ickenham cages, where they were securely locked up for the night. These cages were temporary lock-ups for prisoners awaiting hearings. The Ickenham cage was near the church gate, and until 1831 had been used for Ruislip prisoners until Ruislip built one of its own. The Uxbridge cage erected in 1788 was behind the market house.

The remaining evidence was heard on the following day; however the unnamed male witness promised by Meadows did not appear. The only important new witness was Mary Hill, aged 19, who lived on Ruislip Common near the Six Bells and knew Charles Lamb. On Thursday between ten and eleven o'clock, she was at the upstairs window of her cottage and had seen Lamb, carrying a billhook, walk down the footpath leading to Young Wood, and climb over the stile leading to the wood. After that she had lost sight of him. She went out to visit her grandmother, and around twelve o'clock she again saw Lamb, this time coming down the road from the direction of the wood and the Six Bells carrying a bundle of underwood. She noticed that the

# MURDER AT RUISLIP NEAR UXBRIDGE.

Since Thursday last (the 16th instant) the town and neighbourhood of Uxbridge has been much excited by the sudden and mysterious disappearance of a lad named John Brill, in the employ of Mr. Charles Churchill, an extensive farmer residing at Ruislip, who, it has since been discovered, has been barbarously murdered. It appears that the unfortunate youth, who was 15 years of age, about two months since gave evidence before the Magistrates sitting in Petty Sessions at Uxbridge against two men named Thomas Lavender and James Bray, who were charged with poaching on the grounds of R. Dean, Esq. at Ruislip, on which occasion threats of violence were held out against him by the prisoners and their friends. On Thursday last he left his father's house at Ruislip about a quarter past six o'clock, and proceeded to his master's farm, and about ten o'clock he was set to fill up some gaps in Young-wood. Not returning to the farm in the evening, as was his custom, Mr. Churchill sent to his father's residence to know if he had returned home. His parents replied in the negative, and a search was in consequence instituted with lanterns in the wood, but no trace of him could be discovered. On Friday and Saturday the search was renewed, but with no better success. On Sunday morning a large body of the villagers joined in the search, and about noon the ill-fated youth was discovered by a man named James Lavender, the father of one of the men whom it is alleged had threatened his life, in a hollow in a remote part of the wood. When found he was lying on his back quite dead; his clothes were in disorder, and his face covered with dirt. The mark of a severe blow was discovered under the right ear, from which a quantity of blood had flowed. About six yards behind him the bill-hook which he had been using was found. There were also marks among the decayed leaves for five or six yards as if the deceased had staggered before he fell.

The body was then conveyed to the Six Bells at Ruislip.

At an early hour on Monday morning, in consequence of information which was communicated to T. Dagnall, Esq. he issued warrants for the apprehension of Charles Lamb, Thomas Lavender, and James Bray, jun. on suspicion of having been concerned in the murder. On Tuesday morning Mr. Churchill, Mr. Tobut, and a number of other persons, closely examined the spot where the body was found, for the purpose of ascertaining, if possible, if there were appearances indicating that a struggle had taken place; but, from the wet state of the ground, and the footmarks of the numerous persons who had visited the spot, it was impossible to distinguish the original marks. They, however, during their search, found the cuff and lower part of the sleeve of an old flannel jacket, which had apparently been very recently torn from the arm of some person. They also found a small piece of corduroy at the same spot. Before eleven o'clock numerous persons from Ruislip and the adjacent villages arrived in Uxbridge, and by twelve o'clock the King's Arms was surrounded by a large assemblage. At that hour Sir W. S. Wiseman and T. Dagnall, Esq. the Magistrates, took their seats, when Charles Lamb was ordered to be brought in. The examination was strictly private, and we consequently refrain from publishing the particulars that have been furnished us.

During the examination the Bench signed an order for a *post mortem* examination of the body to take place immediately, and the prisoners were remanded.

*Report of the murder,* County Chronicle, 28 February 1837.

material had some large green pieces in the middle and some on the outside. It was freshly cut.

Mary Brill, sister of the deceased, was 'an intelligent young woman, about 18 years of age'. Confronted with Henry Hill, Mary stated on oath that shortly after Bray and Lavender were charged with poaching Henry had come to her and said, 'Tell Jack to look out, for Jem Bray says he'll kill him as soon as he has an opportunity.' When she returned home she told her mother and brother about it, but John had only smiled and said he 'did not care for Jem Bray.'

Henry Hill was questioned but denied that he had ever said the words to Mary. It is tempting to suppose that the fate of John Brill had left him too terrified to say anything.

Charles Lamb was given the opportunity of saying something in his defence. He asserted his innocence, but acknowledged that what Mary Hill had said about his movements on the Thursday was correct. He named the fields he had crossed over between the times of Mary's two sightings, and also gave the names of several people to whom he had spoken while doing so, but none of these potential witnesses were called to prove his alibi.

The magistrates told Lamb that there were two very suspicious circumstances against him, the first being that he was the only person who had been seen going

*The graveyard, St Martin's parish church.*

*Old cottages, Ruislip.*

to and from the wood that day and also that it was between the hours of ten and twelve, when the murder was thought to have taken place. Why the magistrates had decided that the murder had been committed before midday is not known and they were to contradict themselves almost immediately afterwards. Lamb was again remanded, and James Bray brought into the court.

The evidence was read over to Bray after which he stated that he was entirely innocent, and called two witnesses, George Allday and Thomas Godliman, to prove where he was all day Thursday. Allday was a 24-year-old labourer of Ruislip Common, and Godliman was a 27-year-old small farmer who lived not far from the Brills. What they said is not recorded but the magistrates told Bray that the evidence of these witnesses did not do away with the suspicions against him. They now suggested that the boy might not have been murdered on the Thursday but on the Friday or even the Saturday, and might have been secreted somewhere all that time. The magistrates therefore felt they would not be doing their duty if they discharged him. Bray was remanded. Finally Thomas Lavender was brought in. There was no further evidence against him and the magistrates, after a long consultation, discharged him on his promise to appear again when called upon.

An order was signed for a post-mortem examination to take place immediately. Just as the prisoners were being removed, a Bow street officer called Shackle arrived to assist in prosecuting inquiries into the affair. There being considerable demands on the time of Mr Stirling the coroner, it was thought that the inquest would probably not be held until Thursday.

Mr Robert Norton, a surgeon of Uxbridge, performed the post-mortem on 21 February and concluded that the cause of death was a blow or blows of considerable violence from a flat instrument. The side of a billhook could have produced the injuries.

The inquest was held on the Wednesday and Dagnall and Wiseman were in attendance. Charles Lamb's daughter, Sarah, who lived close to Young Wood, told the court that she had heard the scream of 'a big child' as if someone was beating it, at about midday on 16 February. The jury, finding that the evidence against the prisoners was inconclusive, returned a verdict of 'wilful murder against some person or persons unknown'. Under the circumstances the magistrates had no alternative but to discharge all three.

After the prisoners' handcuffs were removed, young Bray begged a favour of the magistrates. He wanted to be permitted to see the body of the murdered boy, saying it would give him pleasure, as he had suffered a good deal through him. Despite the tone of this request it was granted. Some observers felt that Bray had another motive, that he had demanded the test as a means of demonstrating his innocence to the bystanders. It was then a superstition amongst what *The Times* referred to as 'the uneducated classes' that the blood of a murdered person will burst out of the body if it is approached by the murderer. It was directed that all three prisoners should be taken into the room where the body lay. They gazed on the boy's body for a few minutes, and, nothing untoward occurring, they presumably felt that they had made their point. After once again declaring that they were innocent they left. John Brill was probably buried in the graveyard of the parish church of St Martin, but records for that period have not survived. According to local legend, he is buried in the cellar of the Six Bells.

On Wednesday 8 March handbills were received at police offices and station houses offering a reward of £150, £100 of which was provided by the government and £50 by the parish officers of Ruislip to anyone who would give any information which would lead to the apprehension and conviction of the '... persons concerned in the cold-blooded murder of the youth, John Brill'. His Majesty's free pardon was offered to any accomplice in 'the horrid deed' who had not actually assisted in the murder, who gave such information.

Despite every effort made by the local authorities to trace the murderer, no further information emerged. The families of the bereaved, the accused and the witnesses, living cheek by jowl in what *The Times* called 'the rural and retired parish of Ruislip', had to get along as best they could.

Charles Lamb continued his criminal career. He was in court again on 27 February 1837 charged with stealing a ewe. The animal had been cut up and partly cooked so identifying it was difficult. He was acquitted. He was then living with 24-year-old Charlotte Bray (presumably a member of the extended Bray family of Ruislip). On 18 June 1838 he and Thomas Brill the younger, the 40-year-old son of a Ruislip farmer, were indicted for stealing 700lbs of bark. Found guilty, Lamb was sentenced to seven years transportation. He served four years aboard a prison hulk at Portsmouth before

*Coldbath Fields House of Correction, 1814.*

receiving a pardon and returned to the neighbourhood of Ruislip. He and Charlotte were married in March 1842. On 14 October 1844 he was convicted of poaching, sentenced to six months in prison and committed to Coldbath Fields House of Correction. On the same day an associate of his, 25-year-old George Sibley, was convicted of a similar offence and was also imprisoned for six months.

George Sibley, the son of a farmer's labourer, was born in Harefield only two and half miles from Young Wood. He had been married for six years and was making a living by doing odd jobs such as digging gardens, supplementing this meagre income with petty crime. He had previously served four short prison terms for poaching and fishing and had once been charged with stealing money but had been discharged.

On 22 December 1844 Sibley asked to see the chief warder, Mr Hoare, as he had something of importance to say. When Hoare arrived demanding 'What's the matter?' Sibley said, 'Charles Lamb told me of a murder.' Sibley was taken before the governor, Mr G.L. Chesterton, and made a statement, as a result of which Chesterton called Lamb into his office on the following morning. Without telling the prisoner of the charge against him, Chesterton asked him if he had ever known John Brill. He watched Lamb's face carefully but was unable to detect any emotion at the mention of the name. Lamb admitted that he had been arrested on a charge of murdering Brill, adding, 'Thank God, I am clear of that.'

That afternoon, Chesterton wrote a letter to Sir William Wiseman. Sibley had told the governor that one afternoon about a fortnight before their committal, he and Lamb had been travelling on the road from Rickmansworth to Harefield when Lamb had told him that a few years ago he had killed a boy called Brill in Mr Churchill's wood. Sibley added that Lamb had said he had committed the murder by striking the lad on the head with a stick. He had then hung the boy's cap on a branch to make it appear that he had fallen out of a tree and left the boy's billhook and glove lying near the body. According to Sibley, Lamb, having made this damaging confession, had then warned him that if he should tell a word of it to anyone it would be the worse for him.

Sibley had asked the chief warder whether, if he was to give the information, he would get his liberty, so his motives for making the statement were highly suspect but it could not be ignored. 'This is a suspicious circumstance,' wrote Chesterton, 'but I have thought it desirable to put you, as one of the local magistrates, in possession of what has been stated to me. You may send any person whom you may think fit to sift the matter.'

Chesterton advised that he intended, at the next meeting of the visiting justices, to inform them of what he had been told so that they could take any action they thought necessary; concluding, 'I must add, from my observation of Sibley, I do not attach much credit to his statement.'

Immediately on receiving Chesterton's letter Wiseman got in touch with the other Uxbridge magistrates, and it was agreed that on the following Saturday Wiseman and Dagnall should go to the House of Correction to take Sibley's deposition. The confrontation took place on 28 December 1844 and, having sworn Sibley in the presence of Lamb, they took a statement.

Sibley said that he had known Lamb well for over a year and had always been on good terms with him. Three months ago he and Lamb had both been convicted of poaching, and 'being ordered to be sent to prison for it, were at hide and seek together' to avoid the officers.

Early in October they had been walking along the road from Rickmansworth to Harefield between four and five o'clock in the afternoon, talking about how easily and quickly they could get into trouble, but how hard it was to get out of it again. Lamb commented, 'I have heard that the House of Correction is a bad prison; you have been, how is it?' Sibley said it was 'bad enough' to which Lamb replied, 'I would sooner be taken for my murder than I would go there.'

'Murder?' said Sibley, upon which Lamb said, 'I went to get a bundle of wood in Mr Churchill's wood, and a boy came round the wood by the name of John Brill, and he saw me, and he came up to me, and I took and struck him and knocked him down; so I stood a few minutes, and I hung his cap up in the bushes, and his bill and his cuff I chucked down aside of him, making believe as if he had tumbled out of a tree.' Lamb added, 'there is no one knows of it but you and me, and if I happen to hear that you tell anyone, I will kill you.'

Sibley said that his reason for making the statement was because he had had 'such queer dreams' and could not sleep on account of his knowledge of the murder. While both men were out of prison he had felt that he was in danger of his life if he said anything, but now that Lamb was in prison he thought he could tell his story without danger of reprisal. He admitted that he had heard about the murder at the time it happened and had known that Lamb had been arrested for it.

Lamb asked Sibley if he could look him in the face and say that he told him such a thing, but Sibley was adamant; 'That you certainly did,' he said, adding that he had told nothing but the truth and his story was as true as he stood there. He claimed that the statement had been made voluntarily and that no one had held out any promise or favour to him in return.

Lamb treated the matter stoically, and when the deposition had been completed, stated, 'All the statement made by George Sibley is untrue.'

On 30 December a letter was sent on behalf of the Justices of the Peace for Uxbridge to the Secretary of State for the Home Department, enclosing a copy of Chesterton's letter and Sibley's deposition. It was hoped that the Home Office would make an order for the prisoners to be brought to Uxbridge so that they could appear before the magistrates to be examined. The reply was disappointing. Sir James Graham the Home Secretary responded on 31 December. He did not wish to make an order for the two men to be removed from Coldbath Fields and taken to Uxbridge, and suggested that the Uxbridge magistrates make their examination in the prison. This left the county of Middlesex with the expense of conveying all the witnesses from Uxbridge to London, instead of the relatively small expense of bringing the two prisoners to Uxbridge.

On the news becoming known, considerable excitement swept through the western and north western regions of Middlesex. On 4 January the magistrates mustered all the witnesses who had given evidence at the inquest on John Brill and at the magistrates' hearings at the Kings Arms Inn, for the purpose of taking their statements to see how much they recalled. The public crowded around the outside of the inn, in the belief that some decision was imminent, and on 6 January, when the court of petty sessions was held, the magistrates' room and the road outside the inn were again crowded in the expectation that a public examination of the matter would take place.

On 21 January Lamb appeared before Middlesex magistrate Mr C. Mills. The main evidence against him was that of Sibley who repeated his story, saying that he had felt he could not be happy until he had told what he knew, and thought something might happen to him if he did not. Asked to look Lamb in the face and declare that he had told the truth, Sibley did so unflinchingly.

Lamb protested his innocence saying that Sibley had only told the story so he might be released from prison. He pointed out that Sibley had been living in the neighbourhood at the time of the murder, and knew all the details. Charles Lamb was committed to take his trial at the Central Criminal Court, Old Bailey for the murder of John Brill. He was charged on two counts; that of killing Brill with an iron bill, but also, probably because the actual weapon had not been identified, with committing murder with 'a certain offensive weapon to the jury unknown'.

The trial opened on Friday 7 February, but Lamb's counsel, Mr Wilkins, at once rose and asked if the hearing might be postponed another day. The prisoner, he said, 'was a man of destitute circumstances and without means', and but for the benign interference of the Sheriff's counsel he would not have been instructed to defend him. He was therefore wholly unprepared to enter upon the case. He had only received the brief very late on Wednesday and had spent most of Thursday in the Court of Exchequer. The trial was postponed until 10 a.m. the following morning, when Lamb was brought to the bar before Mr Baron Parke and Mr Justice Williams.

James Lavender told the court that he remembered the events of 1837 very well, but oddly he is recorded as saying that he did not think one of his sons was taken before the magistrate, and was unable to recall if the son was sent to the cage. He had had five sons, one of whom had been 'killed in fighting about five years ago' (he may have been referring to the first Anglo-Afghan war 1839–42) and Thomas had 'gone for a soldier'. He explained his rapid finding of the body by stating that he knew the wood well, and seeing the other men going along a broad path said to himself, 'This is not the way I used to go when I went a bird-nesting' and had gone off on his own on a different path.

A new witness, Ruislip farmer Charles Woodman, said that he had seen John Brill at eleven o'clock on 16 February hard at work in the meadow.

Henry Woodman, who had been twelve at the time of the murder, had been near Young Wood on 16 February at eleven o'clock when he saw Lamb on the road about 20 yards from the wood. Lamb asked Woodman if Churchill and his wife had gone to market that day, and Woodman replied that they had gone about an hour or an hour and a half ago. He was sure that Lamb was not carrying anything.

Labourer John Bray, the brother of Charles Lamb's wife, had been coming from Woodcock's Hill to Ruislip at about twelve o'clock, when he met Lamb walking down a footpath across a meadow about a mile from Young Wood. Lamb was walking at a rapid pace, and was sweaty and warm. Bray asked Lamb where he was going and Lamb said he was looking for some briars. He carried neither billhook nor wood. The two men went to the Six Bells together for some beer.

Surgeon Robert Norton confirmed that a billhook could have caused the boy's injuries, which could not have been the result of a fall from a tree on soft ground. He had examined the spot where the body had lain and there was no stump of a tree there. The overhanging bough at its junction with the tree was the thickness of his arm and above the place where the body lay it was no thicker than his thumb. The boy was 'a stout boy' he added.

The star witness was George Sibley, who had been brought to court from the House of Correction. The defence did its best to discredit him, establishing that he subsisted on very little income, and suggesting that he had given the information in the hope of a reward. Asked what his wife did for a living when he was in gaol, he said he didn't know and rejected the accusation that she was working as a common prostitute.

Mr Wilkins tried to persuade the court that it was possible that the boy had died accidentally by falling out of the tree, but said that even supposing he had been murdered the injury could have been made with the butt of a poacher's gun. He did not think it likely that Lamb would have walked so calmly down the road if he had just committed a murder. The only evidence against him was that of Sibley and his motive was obviously to get out of prison and also the reward money. Wilkins exhorted the jury to give the prisoner the benefit of the very grave doubt 'with which this case was crowded.'

Mr Baron Parke told the jury that the case rested almost entirely on the word of Sibley. If they believed him they would find the prisoner guilty. It was for them to judge Sibley's motives for coming forward. He added that in his opinion the weight of evidence was against the theory of the boy having fallen out of the tree. After half an hour's deliberation the jury acquitted the prisoner.

Lamb was unable to stay out of trouble. In 1849 he was sentenced to fourteen years' transportation at St Alban's Quarter Sessions for stealing bark. He served part of the sentence at Portsmouth and had been out on a nine-month ticket of leave when, in 1854, he was back at the Old Bailey on a charge of stealing hay for which he was given six months in prison. His subsequent fate is unknown.

George Sibley returned to his wife Maria, and continued to work as an agricultural labourer. He died in 1881.

The mystery of the murder of John Brill remains unsolved.

# 4

# IN THE HEAT OF THE MOMENT

## *Hillingdon, 1839*

In March 1839 19-year-old Francis Hastings Medhurst was a young man with excellent prospects. Francis' father, William Granville Hastings Medhurst, a direct descendant of the 7th Earl of Huntingdon, was an Army officer who had served in Italy, where he married Fortunata Pappalardo in 1814. Francis was their eldest son, born on the family estate of Kippax Hall near Leeds, but the family moved to Italy when he was six months old. William died in 1835, and shortly afterwards the family returned to England.

Francis was poised to inherit a fortune of £7,000 on the death of his grandfather, stockbroker and landowner Granville William Wheler Medhurst. There was, however, another legacy which he may have already inherited from that relative. Granville Medhurst suffered from mental instability which led to violent rages. 'From a boy,' wrote *The Gentleman's Magazine*, 'Mr M. was wild, eccentric, and unaccountable. He had an uncle who was insane, and other relatives who had occasionally shown marks of incoherency.'

Granville had married Sarah Ann Jennings in 1778, 'a lady of the most amiable disposition,' and the couple had eight children of whom six survived infancy. In April 1800, with Sarah again heavily pregnant, Granville's behaviour became so erratic that it gave rise to considerable anxiety. He was obsessed with the notion that people were plotting against him to get his property and in particular that his wife was planning to poison himself and the children. Sarah was convinced that he would never harm her, but on 4 May he stabbed her to death with a sword. The savagery of the attack, the numerous wounds and the fact that the fatal one had been in the neck gave rise to a rumour that he had actually severed her head from her body. If true, this was not reported at the time. Granville made no attempt to escape, and the house was surrounded while a servant managed to take the children to safety. Eventually Granville was arrested and tried for murder at York assizes, but was acquitted on the grounds of insanity, and ordered to be confined, with his estate being placed in the hands of managers. In 1830 it was decided to move him to a more southerly climate for the sake of his declining health, and he was placed in Messrs Stillwell's lunatic asylum at Moorcroft House, Hillingdon, a privately owned establishment for the care of the insane, most of whose inmates were of the middle and upper classes.

Since January 1837, Francis Medhurst had been a pupil of Revd Frederick Sturmer, curate of the parish of Hayes, who was the principal of a small school at the rectory, Wood End Green. Sturmer, who was born about 1804, had been appointed curate in 1835 and occupied the rectory with his wife Ann and their three children. By 1838, Francis had completed his education but stayed on as a lodger. There were then two other pupils, both about 18, Maximilian Dalison and Edward William Bunney. On 13 February 1839, a new boy, 18-year-old Joseph Alsop, joined the school. Alsop was, like Medhurst, a young gentleman of property. An orphan, he was under the guardianship of an aunt who lived in Tottenham. Medhurst was hot-tempered and quarrelsome, and Alsop enjoyed schoolboyish taunts, so it was not long before the two were on bad terms.

At about 10 a.m. on the morning of Saturday 9 March, Maximilian Dalison was due to set out on a journey and had just left the rectory on his way to order a coach. Sturmer was in the parlour with Alsop and Bunney, who were getting the books they needed to commence their studies, when Medhurst walked in. He was in his dressing gown, and carried a thick walking stick in one hand and a watch in the other.

*Moorcroft House. The central section is Georgian, flanked by Victorian additions.*

Medhurst, his face grim with anger, strode up to Sturmer. 'See what a blackguard has just left your house,' he exclaimed, showing the curate the watch. 'See, he has broken the glass of my watch.' Sturmer was sympathetic, for he knew that the watch was an item Medhurst valued highly as it had belonged to his deceased father, but Alsop turned round to defend Dalison. 'You are a liar and a blackguard for saying so,' he told Medhurst.

In a sudden flash of rage Medhurst struck out with his stick, the first blow hitting Alsop across the left temple, the second striking his shoulder. Alsop flung up his arms to protect himself and was hit again on his right wrist. Alsop, who was both taller and stronger than Medhurst, leaped from his chair and closed with him. A scuffle ensued, the two boys fighting for possession of the stick. Revd Sturmer, faced with an open conflict between two of his charges, then did something that he would regret for the rest of his life. Making no attempt to separate them, without even a verbal remonstration, he rose and left the room. As Edward Bunney stared at the two protagonists, Alsop succeeded in wresting the stick from Medhurst. For a few seconds the boys faced each other, some 6–8ft apart, getting their breath back, then Alsop advanced, raising the stick in both hands to hit Medhurst. As he did so, Medhurst pulled a spring knife from his pocket, flicked out the blade, strode forward and stabbed Alsop in the abdomen. Alsop immediately clutched his hands to his belly, and, crying out, 'he has stabbed me, he has stabbed me', fell against the mantel-piece, and then collapsed onto his knees on the rug. Medhurst ran from the room.

Sturmer was returning to the parlour when he saw Medhurst emerging in a great hurry, his face ghastly pale, muttering 'Good God!' At first the curate thought it was

*The Church of St Mary the Virgin, Hayes, 1873.*

Francis who had been injured. He was about to enter the room when he saw Alsop stagger out, leaning on one side, saying he was injured. According to Sturmer's later statement he immediately ran and told his servant to get a doctor, but this claim is not borne out by other evidence. In fact from this moment on, all of the Revd Sturmer's account of the incident is a desperate and sometimes demonstrably untruthful attempt to show himself in the best possible light and should therefore be regarded with some caution.

When Bunney had recovered from his shock his first impulse was to get away, and without making any attempt to help Alsop, he ran out of the house calling for Dalison to come back. Dalison had not gone far and turned to speak to him. Sturmer also ran after Dalison telling him to return, but when the boy learned what had happened, he refused. Neither Bunney nor Dalison re-entered the rectory that day, Dalison continuing with his journey and Bunney being later traced to his father's house in Newbury, where he said he had run away because he was afraid.

John Rose, the Sturmers' footman, was in the stable a few yards away at the time of the stabbing but hearing a commotion, he started back and saw Dalison walking away from the house, Bunney rushing out after Dalison and Sturmer following Bunney. Rose found Alsop in the hallway clutching his abdomen, being supported by Francis Medhurst. Medhurst then helped the wounded boy upstairs to his bedroom. Rose followed them and found the bedroom door fastened, but when he tried to open it Medhurst unlocked it. Medhurst, who looked very frightened, told Rose, 'Fetch Dr Chadwick.'

Local practitioner Benjamin Chadwick lived only minutes away. He arrived to find Alsop lying on his bed and Medhurst leaning over him, pressing a napkin firmly to the wound to try and stop the flow of blood.

The initial examination showed that there was a single wound on the left side an inch below the navel, and about an inch and half in length. It was a gaping transverse incision through which the surface of the peritoneum could be seen. 'Is it mortal?' asked Alsop. Chadwick, believing that no internal organ had been punctured, said it was not. He decided to put in a suture to hold the edges together; but not having a surgical suture with him, he used an ordinary needle supplied by Mrs Sturmer which he passed through the skin and muscle of the wound winding it around with sewing silk. He then applied a plaster and a bandage, the dressings also being supplied by Mrs Sturmer.

According to Chadwick, the Revd Sturmer was not in the room during the examination or treatment, although he may, as he claimed, have gone back and forth with medical supplies, but Medhurst remained present the whole time, and was so anxious and attentive that Chadwick believed the two boys to be on friendly terms. When the wound was dressed Medhurst said, 'Thank God it is no worse' and he and Alsop both said that they were sorry for what had happened. As he left, Chadwick told the Sturmers that it was only a superficial wound.

The news of the stabbing soon came to the notice of local constable Thomas Clarke, who went to the rectory and spoke to Medhurst. Francis admitted that he had cut another pupil while in a great rage and he was very sorry for it, but said that the doctor had given his opinion that there was no danger. He asked Clarke if he should go away for a week but Clarke told him to remain in case anything serious should occur.

When Sturmer came to see the boys he found Alsop in bed and Medhurst by his side. 'We were both wrong,' said Alsop, 'I forgive you.' Alsop asked if his aunt could be sent for as she was 'almost a mother to him' but Sturmer suggested that this could wait until the next day. Alsop shook his head and said that he might not be alive the next day and Medhurst offered to pay for the cost of an express messenger. Eventually the message was sent and Alsop's aunt arrived that same evening.

Chadwick returned to see his patient at 4 p.m. and found him comfortable. Alsop complained only of a sore head from the blow, and constipation, for which Chadwick said he would send purging pills and a mixture. At 10 p.m. Chadwick was back at the rectory and found the patient more comfortable, the laxatives having had their effect. Chadwick told Alsop's aunt and the Sturmers that he hoped the boy would recover in a few days. There was no fireplace in the room and Chadwick suggested that Alsop should be placed in more comfortable accommodation. Medhurst immediately suggested that Alsop should be transferred to his room, where there was a fire, and this was done.

On the Sunday morning Mrs Sturmer sent a note to Chadwick saying that Mr Patten, an Uxbridge surgeon, had been called in. It was never explained why a second doctor had been called, but it might have been at the request of Alsop's family. Alsop was not complaining of any pain from his wound, but felt some tightness in his abdomen that must have given cause for concern. The two doctors met to discuss the case, and Patten insisted on seeing the wound for himself, removing the bandages which Chadwick had intended should remain in place another day. Although Chadwick thought the wound was knitting Patten thought it was inflamed, and decided to remove the needle. In Chadwick's own words: 'The needle being then rusty, required a good deal of force to drag it out, the hole not having been enlarged by suppuration, and on its being got out, a part of the wound opened.' Patten ordered a poultice and leeches. Over the next few days the tenderness of the abdomen increased and there was persistent vomiting. More leeches were applied on the Monday morning, when it was seen that the edges of the wound were tinged with blue. Alsop remained constipated and Patten administered 'black draught', a laxative mixture composed amongst other things of senna and Epsom salts. The patient seemed a little better on the Tuesday morning but that evening the vomiting became more violent. Another black draught was administered. At the Wednesday morning visit the doctors found that the boy had been vomiting all night, filling two wash hand basins with matter of a yellow, black and green colour, and the stomach was enlarged and swollen. It was apparent to them that the boy was dying. Dr Patten asked to see the knife that had inflicted the wound, and Francis gave it to him. Another doctor, Ralph Frogley of Hounslow, arrived, and told Alsop that his case was hopeless. The boy said that he forgave Medhurst. On Thursday morning, with his uncle and three aunts by his bedside, Alsop was too ill to speak. He died shortly after midday.

Sturmer did not choose to report the incident to the authorities, and Alsop had declined to make any charge against Medhurst, but the local police must have been keeping an eye on the situation. Two constables of the mounted patrol called Messing and Kelly, reported the death to a local magistrate, Count de Salis, who ordered Medhurst's arrest.

At the post-mortem, which was carried out by Dr Chadwick on the morning of Saturday 16 March, it was found that the wound was 2 inches deep and had penetrated the peritoneum.

On Friday 15 March, Francis Medhurst was brought before the Uxbridge magistrates, Count de Salis, Thomas Dagnall, Sir William Saltonstall Wiseman Bt., and T.T. Clark junior, at the magistrates' room of Kings' Arms Inn. He maintained his self composure during questioning, and listened to the evidence very attentively, but left all comments to his solicitor Mr Ludlow and his counsel, the unfortunately named Mr Stammers. The magistrates were particularly interested to know why Revd Sturmer had left the room when the fight started. Sturmer could only manage the weak explanation 'the prisoner was a gentleman of very hasty temper and I knew it was no use interfering at that time.' When Sturmer was censured for not reporting the stabbing, he claimed that he had acted under legal advice but did not say whose. Francis was taken by fly (a light carriage) to the station house at Windsor Street, Uxbridge, where he was placed in the charge of Sergeant Cooper, formerly of the A Division of the Metropolitan Police. It was reported that the prisoner slept well that night.

The inquest commenced in the parlour of Mr Sturmer's residence, at 12 noon on Saturday 16 March before the coroner Mr Wakely MP. The jury consisted of seventeen respectable inhabitants of Hayes, including Mr Chadwick Jones the barrister, while Mr Churchwarden Eve was chosen as foreman. The body of Joseph Alsop lay in an upstairs room and only the coroner, jurors and medical men were permitted to view it. By the time they had all returned, so many onlookers had crowded into Mr Sturmer's parlour that it was decided to adjourn the proceedings to the larger accommodation of the Adam and Eve Inn.

The evidence of Edward Bunney, the only witness to the stabbing, was of especial interest. He revealed that Medhurst and Alsop had quarrelled at the dinner table the previous Sunday because Alsop had taken a hassock at church which Medhurst had wanted. Medhurst had accused Alsop of treating him as a boy and Alsop called Medhurst a blackguard. They had also had a quarrel earlier in the week. Bunney had first seen Medhurst with a knife about a month before the stabbing, and Medhurst had often said that if he was ever worsted in a fight he would stab the other party. Three weeks previously he had quarrelled with Dalison, who offered to fight him with fists, but Medhurst replied that there was 'such a thing as stabbing a person'. Since that day Medhurst had not been on speaking terms with Dalison, and from the Sunday before the stabbing the same coldness had extended to the other two boys. Sturmer, said Bunney, had made no effort to reconcile the parties, and took Medhurst's part against the other boys. Indeed Bunney was of the opinion that the household was split into two distinct factions, Medhurst and the Sturmers against the others.

Asked about Medhurst's general character, Bunney said, 'I dare say there were faults on both sides. We could not agree; he had such nasty sneaking ways, telling everything.'

It was not possible to hear all the evidence in one day, and the proceedings were adjourned. Alsop's body was placed in a coffin, and under the coroner's order taken in a hearse from the house of Mr Sturmer to the residence of the aunt in Tottenham Green, where he was interred in the vaults of the parish church on the following day.

Confined at the station house, Medhurst's earlier equanimity had vanished, and he became very restless. When he was told what facts had been given in evidence at the inquest, and of the adjournment, he became very depressed, and prayed fervently at frequent periods through the night.

On the Sunday Mr Sturmer sent him some books which he hoped might divert him, amongst which were a romance, and a list of novels with which he might be supplied. Francis, however, felt no inclination for light reading, and may also have appreciated what Sturmer clearly did not, that the book choices were wholly inappropriate to his situation. He asked Cooper for a Bible and a prayer book, which he studied diligently.

On Monday 18 March Uxbridge was crowded with people eager to hear Medhurst's re-examination. The magistrates took their seats at 11 a.m., and the large justice room in the yard of the King's Arms Inn was crowded to suffocation. The throng was doomed to disappointment however, for the inquest not having been completed the examination had been postponed.

At the reconvened inquest Sturmer revealed that he too had known about Medhurst owning a knife, which he used for cutting string or for carpentry. Speaking of the factions that had arisen at the rectory, he said that Alsop usually took Dalison's side when there was a dispute between him and Medhurst. He described Francis as having 'a warm Italian temperament'. The coroner took a dim view of Sturmer's failure to properly supervise his pupils and asked him for an explanation of his behaviour when Alsop and Medhurst were fighting. Sturmer's second attempt was even feebler than the first: 'I was so taken by surprise. I did not know what to do. I left the room to know what I was to do.' He admitted that he had not called anyone in to try and separate the boys.

Bunney remembered another detail and was recalled. When Medhurst had first complained to Sturmer that Dalison had broken his watch, Sturmer had commented, 'I wonder you have not knocked him down before.' Medhurst replied, 'I should have done so, only I was afraid to dirty my hands.' The magistrates recalled Sturmer and asked him what he had said to Medhurst. When Sturmer said he believed he had made no answer, Bunney's evidence was read over to him. The curate then said that he couldn't remember the comment but in justice to Bunney he might have made it and forgotten in his confusion. Sturmer then became so agitated that at the suggestion of the coroner he retired from the room.

John Rose, the Sturmers' footman, revealed further details which did not reflect well on the curate. On the Wednesday night Sturmer had been preparing Medhurst's escape, for Rose had been sent to order a fly for 8 the next morning but this instruction had then been countermanded. On Thursday morning, with Alsop sinking fast, Mrs Sturmer sent Rose to order a fly at once, and when Rose returned soon after midday he learned that Alsop had just died. Sturmer and Medhurst took the fly and departed. Rose confirmed that he had seen Medhurst with the knife prior to the stabbing. He had shown it to the Sturmers and the other pupils demonstrating how he could open it in an instant to defend himself.

The next witness was Joseph Baylis, the landlord of the Adam and Eve public house. He and his wife had spoken to Sturmer between 12 and 1 p.m. on the day of the stabbing and asked him whether he had seen the incident. Sturmer had said, 'No, I did not, for when the first blow was given I left the room, as I considered he [Mr Medhurst] was serving him right.' At last Sturmer's strange behaviour was explained. Having seen the blow with the stick he had decided to leave the room to allow Medhurst to deliver a thrashing to Alsop which he must have felt was deserved and which he himself was unwilling to administer.

The unfortunate curate was again called back before the coroner and Baylis' evidence was read out to him. He tried to explain it away by saying he had been misunderstood. Sturmer admitted that on the day Alsop died he had taken Medhurst to the house of a magistrate, Mr Clark of Ickenham, but Clark had said he could not interfere in the case until after a coroner's inquest had sat. As they left Clark's they had been met by a patrol on horseback which stopped them. Sturmer had asked by whose authority they were being stopped and the reply was the magistrate, Count de Salis, and they had been taken to Count where Sturmer was obliged to surrender his charge.

As soon as the inquest jury had retired, Messrs Stammers and Ludlow proceeded in a post-chaise from Hayes to Uxbridge to see their client. The jury took over an hour to reach a majority (fifteen to two) verdict of wilful murder against Francis Medhurst. One point they were unanimous upon was that the conduct of the Revd Sturmer was 'highly reprehensible'.

During the afternoon, the excitement having somewhat died down, Francis was brought before the Count de Salis where, unable to bear the suspense, he implored to be told the jury's verdict at the earliest possible moment. Francis had mentally prepared himself for a verdict of wilful murder against him and when he was advised of this he did not seem greatly surprised. He was remanded until Tuesday.

Soon afterwards he received a visit from Mr Sturmer. That night Medhurst was observed very closely, two constables sitting up with him, and towards morning he was in tears.

On 21 March the Uxbridge magistrates committed a weeping Francis Medhurst to be tried at the Old Bailey on a charge of manslaughter. Sturmer was now claiming that Francis and Alsop had been on good terms before the Sunday quarrel, and that he and his wife had tried several times to reconcile them. There was no evidence to support this statement. Medhurst was removed to Newgate to await his trial.

After the murder some newspapers carried a lurid and imaginative account of the murder of Francis' grandmother. It was claimed that Granville, after cutting off his wife's head, placed it on a table and said, 'There, now, will you hold your tongue!' – a story which was later denied. Granville, in his mid-seventies and in poor health, had not been told of the charge against his grandson.

When the news of Medhurst's arrest became known in Italy, the British Consul sent a letter to the authorities in England certifying that the boy's father had died insane.

The trial opened at the Central Criminal Court, Old Bailey on 13 April, before Mr Justice Coleridge and Mr Justice Coltman. Francis, dressed in black and with a dejected expression, was described as 'a young man of slight appearance and dark complexion'. He was allowed to be seated.

Sir Frederick Pollock for the prosecution expressed his regret that Sturmer had left the room, for even if he was no match in bodily strength for his two pupils '... he might have exercised the moral influence he had over them for the purpose of restraining their enmity ...' Showing the knife to the jury he said that it '... was much to be regretted that the law did not provide a punishment to prevent the sale of such weapons and punish persons who should carry them.' Mr Phillips, the Attorney

*Sir Frederick Pollock.*

*Mr Justice Coleridge.*

General, made an impassioned speech for the defence in which he claimed that the prisoner was '... more to be pitied than blamed'; indeed his greatest wrath was saved for the curate who he felt was '... deeply to blame'.

A number of respectable witnesses were called to give the prisoner '... a most excellent character for kindness and generosity of disposition and great humanity.' After an absence of half an hour the jury acquitted Medhurst of murder but found him guilty of manslaughter. Mr Justice Coleridge, in pronouncing sentence, gave due weight to the fact that the crime was unpremeditated. He also advised anyone with knives in their possession to get rid of them as soon as possible. As to Sturmer, '... if he had done his duty as a man, a tutor and above all, a clergyman ...' the catastrophe would never have happened. Francis was sentenced to be imprisoned in Coldbath Fields House of Correction for a term of three years. As hard labour was not included in the sentence, he was allowed to occupy rooms in the house of the prison governor, where books and other comforts were allowed him, and he was able to pursue his interest in carpentry. During his time in prison he showed no signs of mental disturbance and his conduct was considered by the governor to be exemplary.

Many observers felt that Medhurst's rank in society had led to his being given unusually lenient treatment, and his sentence was compared to that in other similar cases, notably the trial of George Coker. In August 1839 Coker, aged 15, stabbed and killed a man called Moses Yates at Hoxton after Yates had struck him three times. Coker had been transported for life.

Mr. Justice Coleridge summed up the case to the jury. He said that the case was one undoubtedly of considerable importance, as well from the situation and rank of life of the prisoner, as from the remarkable circumstances under which the offence charged against him had been committed ; but he did not apprehend that the jury would find so much novelty, or so much difficulty, in the case as those engaged for the defence of the prisoner would lead them to suppose. This case, like all others of a similar description, involved two questions for their decision. First, whether the wound caused the death of the deceased ; and secondly, whether that wound was inflicted by the prisoner, and under what circumstances. Upon the first question they would have to refer to the evidence of the medical men, and upon that he thought there could be no doubt that the fact was as he suggested, and that the argument urged upon their attention by the counsel for the defence, that the death of the deceased was the result of improper treatment, could not be sustained. Upon the second question he thought that the jury would have little hesitation in coming to a determination that the offence—if they should find the prisoner guilty of it—was not of the more serious nature alleged, and did not amount to murder, but at least must be reduced to manslaughter.

The jury retired to consider their verdict at five minutes past five o'clock. After an absence of half an hour's duration, they returned into Court and delivered a verdict of *Acquittal* on the coroner's inquisition, which charged the prisoner with murder, but declared him to be *Guilty* of the minor offence of manslaughter on the bill returned by the grand jury.

The prisoner having been called up for judgment,

Mr. Justice Coleridge proceeded to pass sentence upon him. He said that he had had the advantage of a most able defence, and of a very patient investigation of his case. He rejoiced, from the situation of respectability which the prisoner had held, and from the contrition which he had exhibited up to the present time, that the jury had come to the decision that he was guilty of the offence of manslaughter only ; but he warned him that, for that offence, he was liable to be transported for life. There was one feature in his case which was of considerable weight against him, and which was the possession and use of the knife which had been produced. He most earnestly cautioned all persons in Court to abstain from the purchase of such weapons, and he regretted most sincerely that crimes of this description, resulting from the use of the dagger and the knife, had of late years much increased in this country. He exhorted the prisoner to continue in the course he had already pursued, and to apply the time during which he would be imprisoned to the worship of the Almighty, and in fitting himself on his discharge to fill the position which he was entitled to hold in society. In conclusion the Learned Judge sentenced the prisoner to be imprisoned in her Majesty's House of Correction at Coldbath-fields for the term of three years.

The prisoner is a young man whose appearance is not very prepossessing. He was respectably attired in mourning, and appeared deeply sensible of the situation in which he was placed. He was accommodated with a chair during the trial, which lasted from ten o'clock in the morning. The Court was thronged during the day by respectably-dressed people.

*The conclusion of the trial,* Morning Post, *14 April 1839.*

Revd Sturmer may have felt that with the trial now over, his life would return to normal. He reckoned without the people of Hayes, who shared the views of the court on his conduct. Many of his parishioners began to boycott Hayes' church, choosing instead to travel to Hillingdon and other churches 2 or 3 miles away rather than listen to a sermon from a man in whom they no longer had any confidence. Shortly after the trial a public meeting was held which passed a resolution calling on Sturmer to resign. When he failed to do so, further meetings were held to discuss the best means of getting Sturmer removed from his curacy. Eventually it was agreed that a petition should be sent to the Archbishop of Canterbury quoting the remarks made by the judge and counsel at the trial. The Archbishop replied on 30 May, saying he could find no legal grounds for taking proceedings against the curate. This precipitated another meeting of the parishioners. Weeks passed but the ill-feeling did not abate, despite the strenuous efforts of the rector to effect a reconciliation. In October the rector made one last attempt, arranging a sumptuous dinner with a haunch of roast venison to which he invited the principal inhabitants of Hayes, but when it reached the ears of the parishioners that Sturmer was to be present they declined to attend and in the end only six people dined with the rector and all of those were people who had been most active in promoting the reconciliation.

On 3 April 1840, Granville Medhurst died at the age of 77. On 23 December that year, Francis came of age, and was therefore entitled to take possession of his inheritance of £7,000. He had given no trouble as a prisoner, and was hopeful of an early release. In February 1841 his mother engaged her solicitor to present a petition before the Home Office for a pardon.

In April 1841 an extraordinary rumour came to the attention of the newspapers. It was alleged that Francis had been approached by a visitor suggesting that he could obtain his release from prison on payment of a gratuity of £3,000. This was not to be an escape but a remission of the sentence, and the man who was said to have made the offer, whose identity was known but whose name was not yet made public, was a Middlesex county magistrate who had claimed to have influence with which he could arrange the prisoner's release. Enquiries were at once commenced, and a meeting of the Middlesex magistrates was held on 8 July at which the full details were revealed. The magistrate concerned was Henry Charles Moreton Dyer, who had been removed from the commission of the peace after admitting his indiscretion. Francis had brought the matter to the attention of the prison governor Mr Chesterton in February, saying that a visitor had told him he might obtain an early release for the sum of £3,000. Chesterton told him at once that it was a fallacy to suppose he could obtain his release in that way. Medhurst went on to say he had been advised that it could be done through the influence of Lord and Lady Normanby (Lord Normanby was then the Home Secretary) and Lord Melbourne the Prime Minister. Chesterton replied, 'If there is any object in this proposition, it is to defraud you,' and advised the prisoner not to pay any sum of money. Chesterton naturally demanded to know who had made the proposition, but Medhurst said he had promised not to divulge the name. Chesterton did not take the matter too seriously until he learned from

MIDDLESEX.—*April 3.* At Dr. Still-well's lunatic asylum near Uxbridge, aged 77, Granville William Wheeler Medhurst, esq. of Medhurst-hall, Yorkshire. Of this gentleman some account will be found in the Gent. Mag. for 1800, p. 792; he had been in confinement from that year, when he was tried at York assizes for the murder of his wife, and acquitted on the plea of insanity. His fortune (said to amount to 7000*l.* per ann. and including the township of Kippax) has devolved on his grandson, Francis Hastings Medhurst, now under sentence of three years' imprisonment for the manslaughter of his schoolfellow Joseph Alsop, at Hayes, on the 9th March 1839.

*Obituary of Granville Medhurst in the* Gentleman's Magazine, *1840.*

the prison chaplain that Medhurst had frequently been visited by a magistrate and suspicions hardened when it transpired that Dyer and Medhurst had been overheard talking about the prisoner's release. It was also found that Dyer had claimed he was related to Lady Normanby, which that lady was to deny.

Dyer wrote to the newspapers claiming that his sympathy for Medhurst's plight had led him to suggest that a payment made to a national charity might go in his favour if he was applying for early release, but Medhurst responded that no mention had ever been made of the funds going to a charity.

After some consideration it was decided not to take legal proceedings against Dyer as there was no real evidence that could be brought against him in court. Dyer's correspondence comprising his unconvincing attempts to exonerate himself was published in *The Times* of 10 July 1841. A few days later it was reported that Medhurst had became so depressed that it had been necessary to place him in the prison infirmary. A medical certificate was obtained stating that to keep him in prison any longer might hasten his death. On 24 July he was discharged out of the custody of the governor of the prison under an order from Her Majesty's Secretary of State.

In 1843 Medhurst married Mary Anne Bushnan, the daughter of landed proprietor Charles Osborn Bushnan, eldest son of a former Comptroller of the City of London. The couple must have spent their first years of marriage in Naples as a son and two daughters were born there. They were in London for the birth of another daughter and eventually settled on the family estate at Kippax. Francis died on 4 November 1852, aged 32. The cause of death was given as 'organic disease of the brain' which had been evident for six months. His second son was born in the following May.

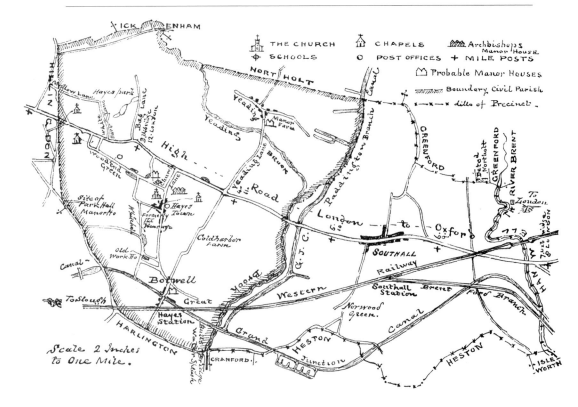

*Sketch map of the parish of Hayes, 1873.*

Revd Sturmer did not prosper. He had tried to carry on as curate of Hayes, despite the boycott, the public meetings, the distrust and the anonymous chalking of slogans on the wall of his house. The vestry, powerless to remove Sturmer from his curacy, retaliated by refusing to pay a church rate, and he had had to meet the considerable expense of upkeep of the rectory. Robbed of the additional income from the school, he had been obliged, in August 1841, to sell off all his furniture, which did not realise enough to pay his debts. In December he appeared before the insolvent debtors' court together with his attorney, Mr Manning, who offered to stand bail for him. The chief commissioner commented that it was a pity the insolvent could not find any of his own personal friends to become responsible for him. 'He has no personal friends,' said Manning. In February 1842 Sturmer again appeared before the court and this time he was remanded to prison.

Sturmer, who later appears in census records as Frederick von Stürmer, eventually obtained a small living, becoming rector of Heapham in Lincolnshire in 1845. He did not take in pupils. In 1849 he was again in debt, and his wife was reduced to writing begging letters. He spent the rest of his life on the edge of bankruptcy, paying off his debts piecemeal, and making several more court appearances. In 1876 he was back in court applying for a stay of a sequestration placed on his living. He died later the same year.

# 5

# THE WINE SHOP MURDER

*Hendon, 1919*

John Thomas Gregory was born in Abingdon, Berkshire on 7 July 1860, the son of Thomas Gregory, a grocer. The family spent some time in Uxbridge, where Thomas worked as a brewer's clerk. In 1881 John was working as an assistant grocer in Marylebone, but by 1891 he had moved to Devon and a position as grocer's manager in Westwell Street, Plymouth. John Gregory married Dumfries-born Isabella Turner in 1894. The family was living in Kingsbridge, Devon, with John managing a grocer's shop in Fore Street, when their two children were born, Sybil Mildred in 1897 and Wilfrid John in 1898. It appears that Gregory and his wife later separated. John Gregory and his daughter came to London in August 1915, where they lived at 90 Warwick Road, Ealing. Wilfrid was then serving in the RAF. In 1916 Gregory obtained a post as manager of an off-license, the Colindale Wine Spirit and Beer Stores, property of Messrs Broad, Wiltshire and Penny. The shop entrance was on Colindale Avenue, but in an adjacent lane there was a side entrance which led to a small sitting room. The licensing laws required that the shop should be shut between 2.30 p.m. and the evening, and Gregory used to spend this time in his sitting room. Although he usually returned home to sleep he sometimes remained at Hendon for the night and did so on Thursday, 3 July 1919.

Between five and ten minutes past five on Friday 4 July, two young women, Barbara Mary Bailey and Florence Wootton, were on their way home from a nearby factory and were passing by the shop when they heard the noise of breaking glass from the sitting room, and what sounded like a violent quarrel. There was a small window in the side lane and Barbara tried to peer inside, but a man in the room quickly pulled the long red curtain across, then used the bottom of the curtain to wipe away what looked like smears of blood on the window pane. She only got a brief glimpse of him, but saw that he was clean shaven and wore a blue coat. Florence did not get such a good look but felt sure that the man was young.

William Tanner, a metal worker of Colindale Avenue, was also passing when he saw the women staring through the window. Going to investigate, he heard groans

SCENF OF THE HENDON MURDER.

The wine store in Colindale avenue, Hendon, where Mr. Gregory, the manager of the store, was brutally murdered a week ago.

*The wine store, Colindale Avenue, in 1919.*

*Mrs Barbara Mary Bailey.*

from inside the sitting room, then breaking glass and sounds 'as if someone was chopping wood on the floor'. Barbara showed him the bloodstained curtain. By now, a small crowd had gathered in the lane. A boy went to the front door and knocked, but there was no response, then Tanner tried to get in through the door but was unable to open it. He peered through the flap of the letterbox and saw the sole of a black boot or shoe, which disappeared down the passage leading to the back of the premises. He then returned to the window, and, peering through it, felt sure he could see a body lying on the floor. He at once went to find a policeman. Another passer-by, Sidney Downes, managed to open the little window. Pulling aside the curtains he saw broken glass on the floor and a man lying in front of the fireplace giving some choking groans. At that moment, Tanner returned with Constable A.S. Cooper who climbed through the window, followed by Downes.

John Gregory, who was suffering from serious head injuries, was still alive, but only moments later he gave two or three gasps and died. Cooper told Tanner to go to the Westminster Infirmary and fetch a doctor. He then made a search of the premises but found no one. A pair of bloodstained coal tongs lay near the body, the grip end broken off. There was also a bent and bloodstained poker. A broken lemon squash bottle also appeared to have been used as a weapon, and pieces of a broken sherry bottle were strewn about the floor.

*Sidney Downes and William Tanner.*

The walls, windows, ceiling and floor of the little sitting room were spattered with blood, as were the curtains at the small window, and the glass panels in the door. There was a piano in the room and its keys were smeared with blood. On the table was a small wine glass and spirit glass, both of which had recently been used, and an overturned flower vase. One chair had been tipped over but that was the only sign that a struggle had taken place. The back door was open, and in the yard a suitcase was found lying between some boxes. It had been raining hard, but the top of the case was only slightly wet, suggesting that it had not been there long.

Dr Toulmin arrived from the infirmary and confirmed that Gregory had been dead for only a few minutes. Constable Cooper remained on the scene until more senior officers, Inspector Lacey and Detective Inspector McEvoy, arrived.

Aubrey Vincent Clark, an apprentice who lodged next door to the wine shop, had seen the murderer escape from the rear of the premises. Based on his sighting the police issued the following description: 'Man, 25 to 30 years of age, height 5ft 8in. to 5ft 10in., clean shaven, medium build, well dressed in navy blue suit, probably serge, permanent turn-up trousers, light grey trilby hat, with broad brim and rather broad black band, and black boots or shoes (American style)'.

Charles Thurston, a discharged soldier, reported that he had seen a man of that description on a bus going in the direction of Golders Green. He had particularly noticed him as there was blood on his forehead and collar.

The shop till was empty, and it was at first assumed that the murder had been committed during the course of a robbery, but it was then discovered that Gregory had already cashed up as the takings were found in a bag. Also in the bag were a

*The finding of John Gregory's body.*

*Aubrey Vincent Clark.*

number of notes. A letter written on a sheet of paper read, 'Dear Old Bean, Called this morning and found you out. Very disappointed. Will call again later in the week, Yours, Cyril.' A card, which looked like a note made for Gregory's reply by telegram, bore the words: 'Staying here tonight. Shall be here tomorrow 9 a.m. Old Bean.' On another card was written: 'Cecil or Cyril Stanley, 29 Russell Square.' The writing on the last card was identified by Gregory's son as his father's. These promising clues however resulted in no new information.

There was only one early arrest. A man was detained by the police in Kings Cross Road because of statements he had made about the murder. He bore no resemblance to the description of the man seen escaping from the wine shop, and the police soon satisfied themselves that he had nothing to do with the murder and released him.

Divisional police surgeon Dr Francis William Andrew examined the body and found that the dead man's nose was broken and there were jagged wounds to the face. The upper jaw was fractured, teeth were broken and there was a wound on the top of the head, which had fractured the skull and exposed the brain. He believed that Gregory had been felled to the ground by a blow on the left side of his head and that the rest of the wounds had been delivered by someone standing over him as he lay on the ground. The tongs, poker and bottles had all been used as weapons.

The inquest was held at Hendon Council offices, Hendon Town Hall, before the coroner, Dr George Cohen, on 8 July. A plan of the premises was produced, and detective sergeant W. McBride of New Scotland Yard showed the jury six photographs, one of which showed the inside of the parlour as it was found by the police, with the battered body of John Gregory lying in front of the fireplace.

Sybil Gregory was shown the large suitcase and a smaller bag found at the scene of the crime. She said that the bag belonged to her father, but she had never seen the suitcase before. It bore the initials J.W.B.

Charles Luthan, who lived next door to the wine store, recalled that about a fortnight before the murder, between five and six one evening, he had seen Gregory walk past in the company of a young man dressed in a blue serge suit and a trilby hat. The man was clean-shaven and about 5ft 9in tall. They had been laughing together.

Aubrey Clark stated that on the night of the murder he had returned home at five past five. Shortly afterwards he had been sitting on a chair at the side of a window, which faced down the garden, stroking a kitten. At 5.20 the kitten suddenly started up, looked down the garden, and sprang across his knees. He looked out of the window and saw a man in a blue suit crossing the lawn, then leaving by the garden gate, which he stooped to unbolt. The man then turned right and walked in the direction of Edgware Road.

After Constable Cooper and Detective Inspector McEvoy had described the scene, the coroner announced that evidence was to follow, the publication of which would hinder the police in their enquiries. He therefore proposed to exclude from the court everyone except the police, the jury and the medical witnesses. The court sat *in camera* for half an hour while evidence of three witnesses was taken. Dr Cohen gave a short summing up in which he stated that the evidence pointed to the man seen in the house being there at Gregory's invitation. The jury returned a verdict of 'wilful murder against some person unknown.' John Thomas Gregory was buried at Ealing cemetery on 10 July.

There was another reported sighting of the man in the blue suit. John Dawe, a bus driver, knew Gregory and on 3 July had seen him board his omnibus with another man. Gregory had alighted at Edgware Road, but the man had travelled on and alighted in Tottenham Court Road near the YMCA.

It soon emerged that J.W.B. was a lodger at the YMCA. His suitcase, marked with his initials, had been borrowed by a young man called Arthur John Biggin, who had abruptly departed for Sheffield the day after the murder. DS Cooper and CI Neil went up to Sheffield to make enquiries, and on 11 July Cooper learned that a young man had been taken to the Royal Hospital after being found in Whiteley Wood, a Sheffield city park, suffering from the effects of poison. He had swallowed cyanide of potassium. Detective Cooper, with Inspector Dyson of the Sheffield police force, identified the patient as the man for whom they had been searching. Potassium cyanide is highly toxic, but Biggin can only have taken a very small dose for he quickly recovered from its effects. 'Yes, I was expecting you,' said Biggin, on learning who his visitors were. 'I tried to take my life because I did not think anyone would believe the circumstances in which I was driven to commit the act.' On the following day Biggin was escorted to London by train.

During the journey Biggin, who may have been made aware that attempted suicide was then a felony under English law, changed his story and claimed that he had not taken the cyanide with the idea of committing suicide. He told the policemen that he had only take a small quantity to see what effect it would produce and was very glad he had not taken enough to end his life. Biggin arrived at

Marylebone station closely guarded but not handcuffed. Walking from the platform amongst the crowds of passengers he went unnoticed.

Arthur Biggin, a tall, slightly built 18-year-old, was the son of Wilfrid John Biggin, a builder and contractor of Ecclesall, Sheffield. Arthur's mother had died in 1902 and he had been brought up by his father and grandparents. It was reported in the newspapers that the previous April he had married a Miss Wesley of Darnall, near Sheffield, and the couple had honeymooned in London. Since the wedding they were said to have been living with his wife's mother. The *Sheffield Independent* described Biggin as 'a youth of bright disposition and good education, very popular with his many friends.'

In Biggin's statement to the police he said he had first met Gregory three weeks previously. He was looking for employment and had an appointment for an interview at Hendon Aerodrome. Alighting from a tram near the Integral Propeller Company, he had asked the way from a gentleman in the street, mentioning that he was going up there seeking a job. The two were then passing the wine shop when the older man said, 'Are you in a hurry?' Biggin said he had to keep an appointment before 12.30. It was then about 11 a.m. 'Would you mind being my guest for a few moments?' said the man. Biggin didn't relate whether he thought there was anything odd about this request from a stranger. According to his statement he replied, 'I don't mind coming in for a few moments.'

Gregory – for it was he – took his guest into the wine shop through the side door. Biggin sat down, was given a cigarette, and his host got out a bottle of wine. Biggin, who admitted that he knew very little about wine, thought it might have been port. He told his new friend that he was not in the habit of drinking a great deal, but accepted a glass. They chatted, Biggin giving his name as Cyril Stanley, with an address in Richmond Square, details which the shop keeper noted down on a card. The stay lasted a quarter of an hour, after which Biggin took his leave. 'If you are this way, call again,' said Gregory.

Biggin went on to the aerodrome, where he saw the managing director, Mr Willis, then returned to his lodgings in Tottenham Court Road. A few days later he had a second interview and on the way back he called in on Gregory. He was shown into the back parlour and given a glass of wine. In Biggin's statement the conversation has a curiously stilted and formal air. Gregory said, 'Do you like wine?' to which Biggin replied, 'Yes, it is very nice.' Gregory then said, 'If you care to bring a bag, I will let you have a few bottles.' Biggin thought this a little odd, but as the man was giving him presents saw no reason to refuse. 'I am a comparative stranger to you,' he replied, 'but if you like to make me a present, I shall be pleased to accept it.'

Some days later Biggin had another interview at the aerodrome. On his return he saw that the blinds were down at the shop and assumed that Gregory was not there. He went to a nearby shop for notepaper and wrote a note to say that he had called. The next time he saw Gregory was on Thursday 3 July, when he again went to the aerodrome. If Biggin's account may be accepted then his sole interest in visiting Gregory was the prospect of being given gifts of wine. He had already spoken to some friends, Leslie Feild and Lloyd Goode, telling them that a man was going to give him some wine. On the Thursday he was at the wine shop again and had another drink, which might have been wine, port or sherry. The two men spent some time together then left the shop in each other's company. Biggin was headed back to his lodgings and they got on the bus at Edgware Road. Gregory paid the fare. It was on this journey, according to Biggin, that Gregory's real motives became clear: 'Gregory made overtures to me, which I repulsed. He told me he slept at the shop alone, and asked me if I could arrange to sleep there with him. I did not agree to this.'

Despite this development Biggin agreed to call and see Gregory the next day with a view of getting some wine. On the Friday morning he called at the YMCA on Tottenham Court Road to see Feild and borrowed a suitcase which belonged to a fellow lodger and was initialled J.W.B. After lunching with Feild he left at 1.30 going to Hendon in the No. 1A bus, and arriving at the shop between quarter past and half past two. Biggin went through the shop into the parlour and shortly afterwards Gregory closed up the shop and joined him. Biggin was surprised to see the table laid for a substantial lunch: '... cold meat, pies and sausages on the same dish – all cold – a bottle of pickles, some tomatoes, a large bottle of ale, a bottle of lemonade, and a bottle of sherry.' The table had quite a 'festive' appearance. He asked Gregory if he was expecting someone, and Gregory replied, 'I got it as a surprise for you. I thought you would take lunch with me.' Biggin said he had already had his lunch but Gregory said, 'Never mind, you can take some more.' At this point in his statement Biggin revealed that up to this time he did not know his new friend's name, and it was only during the ensuing conversation that his host told him he was called Gregory. Biggin had a little lunch during which Gregory was keen to press drink on his guest, although Biggin reminded him several times that he was not in the habit of drinking. 'Oh never mind,' said Gregory. 'It will do you no harm.' The two men then tidied away the remains of the meal, Gregory washing the utensils and Biggin drying them.

According to Biggin, Gregory then went to the front of the shop while he relaxed on the couch reading a magazine and enjoying a cigarette. When Gregory returned he had a glass in his hand with a drink of a reddish yellow colour. Biggin asked what it was and his host replied that it was a mixture he had made especially for him. He filled a wine glass for Biggin and also poured a little in a glass for himself.

Biggin drank his. It was heavy and sickly and had a bitter-sweet taste. He remarked that it tasted different from anything he had ever drunk before. 'What have you made this of?' he asked. Gregory, who by now had proved himself the master of the dismissive reply, said, 'Well, it is only an ordinary mixture.' Biggin remained on the couch and soon began to feel heavy and dizzy. Whatever the mixture was it had quite a different effect on him from the wine. Gregory brought a bottle of sherry and poured a glass for Biggin, which he drank, then Gregory sat beside him on the couch. 'He started to tell me some filthy tales, and I took little notice of it because I credited it to the drink.'

According to Biggin's statement Gregory once again made sexual overtures, which he repulsed. He continued to lie on the couch and Gregory gave him some more wine then sat down beside him. 'You young viper, you won't, will you?' he said. 'Then I will make you. If you won't do it, I will make you pay for it.' He then put his hand in one of Biggin's pockets. The young man became alarmed and began to struggle. 'He appeared to go mad, went to the fireplace and got a poker, and made for me as if to strike me with it.' What followed was, in Biggin's account, almost a choreographed fight. Gregory aimed a blow with the poker which Biggin managed to dodge. Biggin grabbed a bottle from the table and hit Gregory over the head with it, breaking the glass. It seemed to have no effect. Gregory still came at him with the poker, and Biggin snatched up the tongs and warded off a series of blows, during which the tongs were broken. He then dropped the tongs, closed with Gregory and managed to get possession of the poker, and hit out with it. Biggin claimed that he had no recollection of what happened after that. He could not remember taking the suitcase outside, but did remember going out of the back door and climbing over the fence into the next door garden. He then unfastened a gate to exit via a passage. He recalled seeing a man looking over a wall or gate and asking him where he could get a bus. As they talked the man lit a cigarette for him. He crossed some fields and finally got a bus to Golders Green, where he took the tube to his lodgings. After a wash and brush up he went to see Goode and told him he was going to Sheffield as he had received a telegram saying that his father was ill. He returned to his lodgings for the night, and after breakfast borrowed £2 from a fellow lodger called Scott, and caught the 8.40 a.m. train from St Pancras to Sheffield, arriving at 5 p.m.

Biggin ended his statement saying that at the time he was struggling with Gregory, 'I felt that if I did not do him in he would do me in.' Claiming he had been 'half dazed' he had decided to get out of London as he thought that if he was caught he might be charged with murder and would have no opportunity of explaining what took place.

On Monday 15 July Biggin was charged at Hendon Police Court with the murder of John Thomas Gregory. Some aspects of the case may have strained credulity. Biggin never claimed that he had not understood what the alleged overtures meant, rather that he knew and had somehow chosen to ignore them even though they disgusted him, and had instead continued to visit the man. Biggin was certainly motivated by the prospect of free gifts of wine, but could he also have been using Gregory's predilections to gain access to the shop with a view to stealing liquor and money? Were the alleged sexual advances only a fabrication to bolster the claim that he had acted in self-defence?

The case for the prosecution was led by Eustace Fulton, junior prosecuting counsel at the central criminal court, who was to go on to have a distinguished career. Fulton was said to have 'an almost uncanny capacity for instinctively getting at once to the heart of a case. In cross-examination he knew exactly what he wanted to get from a witness and having got it never wasted time or spoilt the effect by further unnecessary questions.' Fulton revealed that when Biggin visited the YMCA he had told his fellow lodgers that he had once been a captain in the RAF, which was untrue. The implication was clear: if Biggin had told one lie, what others had he told?

*Miss Sybil Gregory arrives for the inquest.*

*Arthur John Biggin.*

Fulton stated that the first noises to come from the room were those of breaking glass, which must have been the sound of the bottle striking Gregory's head. It was after that event that a man had been seen wiping blood splashes from the window. This meant that the blow with the bottle had been decisive; the assailant would not have closed the curtains and wiped the window while in the middle of a struggle. Yet it was after this incident that men had arrived on the scene and heard sounds like someone chopping wood on the floor. This suggested that what they had heard was Mr Gregory's head being battered as he lay stunned and helpless on the floor.

Fulton pointed out that if Biggin's statement was true, then on 1 July he knew what sort of man Gregory was and what to expect from an invitation to his home. The nature of the blows showed that the force used was greater than needed to protect himself from assault. If a man was attacked he was only entitled to use such force as was necessary to protect himself.

At a subsequent hearing on 25 July, Dr Andrew cast further doubts on Biggin's claims to have had a stand-up fight with Gregory, confirming that the blows with the poker must have been administered while Gregory lay on the floor. Mrs Rosalie Titch identified Biggin as the man who had come into her shop and bought notepaper and envelopes to write a note which he said he was going to 'drop into a friend's letterbox'.

Former soldier Charles Thurston appeared in court with 'wound stripes' on his sleeve, showing that he had been wounded in combat, and identified Biggin as the bloodstained man on the Golders Green bus.

Walker Arrowsmith Scott, an accountant, was Biggin's fellow lodger. Biggin had told Scott that his father was seriously ill in Sheffield, but he did not have the money to go there, and Scott had lent him £2. Leslie Feild, a clerk, confirmed that Biggin had asked for the loan of a bag as he was going to fetch some wine. Biggin had told Feild that half was a gift and half was to be paid for. Biggin's statement to the police had suggested that all the wine was a gift, but he was probably intending to make a profit on it. On 3 July, after he had found the wine shop closed, Biggin told Feild another lie, that he had not been able to take the wine away as his friends were having a party. On the following day Biggin had again asked for a bag and Feild had borrowed J.W.B.'s suitcase. Goode said he had had supper in a restaurant with Biggin on the evening of 4 July. Biggin had not managed to eat all his supper. He looked untidy, which was unusual for him, and there was a dark spot on his shirt front.

Biggin pleaded not guilty to murder and was committed for trial at the Central Criminal Court. On 5 September the medical officer of Brixton Prison certified him as sane.

The trial opened on Monday 15 September before Mr Justice Darling, with Sir Richard Muir and Eustace Fulton prosecuting and John Paul Valetta defending. Muir, aged 62, was one of the greatest Crown prosecutors of his day and was then at the height of his considerable powers. Valetta, 43, had first come to prominence in 1903 with his defence of Samuel Dougal at the Moat Farm murder trial, and he had also acted in the defence of Steinie Morrison in 1911. In both those cases the prisoners had been found guilty.

Before the evidence was heard, Mr Justice Darling said that it was certain that disgusting details would have to be gone into. He asked Muir if it was a case in which any decent woman ought to remain in court listening to it. Muir replied, 'I should not like any woman with whom I was connected to stay in court and listen.' Valetta agreed. Darling observed that there were some women in court and though he did not order them to leave it was obvious that no decent woman would remain. Some women took the heavy hint and left the court.

Muir described the scene of the crime, stating that the bloodstains on the ceiling were 'obviously thrown off from the assailant's weapon in repeated blows.' It was necessary, he told the jury, to see if the prisoner's account of the murder was true. Muir did not dispute Gregory's motive in entertaining Biggin, but did not think that a man of his age could impose his will on an athletic young man. Whatever the right of self-defence, there was an amount of violence which had been continued in circumstances when no defence from the dead man was necessary and no offence from him was possible. All the violence had been on Biggin's side. The prisoner was uninjured and there was no justification for the degree of force he had used.

In court Biggin described what he called his 'life and death struggle' during which Gregory, whom he said was a powerful man, swore at him and pressed him down onto the couch while he had struggled to free himself. He thought that Gregory was losing control, and had a 'very vicious dangerous and abnormal look on his face which very much frightened him.' He said he had no recollection of hitting Gregory while the man was on the floor and could not remember wiping the window. Asked if he was a married man, Biggin said that in April he had run away with a girl and

Clockwise from above left

*Sir Richard Muir.*

*Mr Eustace Fulton.*

*Mr Justice Darling.*

had been living with her ever since. She had remained in Sheffield when he came down to London to look for work and they wrote to each other every day. They had both told their families that they were married and when he went back to Sheffield he continued to live with her. He had tried to get a marriage license but there was a difficulty because they were underage.

'Only up to yesterday morning everyone here was under the impression that you were married,' said Valetta, perhaps not best pleased that his client had been exposed in another lie. Muir cross-examined Biggin about his means of livelihood while living in London, possibly to demonstrate his need of funds since he had been unemployed since coming to London. Whether or not Muir expected the response he received is not known. Biggin said that while in Sheffield, he had been employed by a firm of stockbrokers at wages of 35s a week. He had bought some shares through this firm and had been allowed credit of £2,000 because his family was of good standing in Sheffield and he was due to receive some money when he came of age. Some of the shares had been pledged with an auctioneer for £150 which he used to finance his time in London. Biggin was trying to suggest to the court that his share acquisition was not an illegal transaction, but he had undoubtedly obtained them under false pretences. His father was called to give evidence and said that the shares had been transferred back to the firm except for a few which he had made good.

Although no one had accused Biggin of making up the story of the sexual advances, some doubts may have been in the minds of the jury until Mr Valetta played his trump card. Several young men were called as witnesses, and all testified that Gregory had made overtures to them which they had resisted. They also said that when rebuffed he had become angry and they had been frightened by his appearance. One said he had had a fight with Gregory in which he had thrown four bottles of wine at the older man.

Valetta, in his final address to the jury, said that the defence was that it was a case of justifiable homicide. Muir argued that 'not the smallest credence could be placed on the prisoner's statement in the witness box as he had proved himself a habitual liar and sometimes a motiveless liar.'

The jury found Biggin not guilty of murder but guilty of manslaughter and recommended him to mercy on account of his youth. Mr Justice Darling imposed a sentence of twelve months imprisonment with hard labour. Although he agreed with the verdict he commented that on 4 July the prisoner was not unprepared to hear an improper proposal and '... he knew the class of man he was going to visit.' He commented that if Biggin had been a full grown man, although the man he killed was '... a citizen who could easily be spared ...' the sentence would have been more severe.

An appeal was launched on the grounds that Muir's cross-examination was contrary to section 1 (b) (2) of the Criminal Evidence Act of 1898 in that Biggin had been asked questions which tended to show that he had committed an offence other than that with which he had been charged – the underhand share dealings. On 20 October 1919 the Court of Criminal Appeal quashed his conviction and he was freed.

# 6

# BLAMING A WOMAN

*Golders Green, 1920*

On 12 June 1914, 37-year-old Evelyn Mayer, a widow with three sons, married South African-born Arthur Andrew Clement Goslett, 38. His profession, as described on the marriage certificate, was aeroplane and airship constructor. Later that year he joined the Royal Naval Air Service. A daughter, Leonie, was born to the couple in 1918.

In 1919 the Gosletts were living in an apartment in Armitage Mansions, 85a Golders Green Road. The flat was rented by Mrs Goslett's mother, Mrs Binko, the widow of an Austrian engineer, who kept a servants' registry office at No. 5 Golders Green Parade. The flat was also home to the Gosletts' daughter, the three sons of Evelyn's first marriage, a lodger, bank clerk Francis Hutchinson, and two paying guests, Mrs Marjorie Orrell and her musician husband George. In July another guest came to stay, 26-year-old Daisy, who was introduced as the widow of Arthur's brother Percy. Daisy was seven months pregnant and on 10 September she gave birth to a daughter, Joyce.

On the afternoon of Saturday, 1 May 1920, Evelyn Goslett was in a state of happy anticipation. She told her mother that Arthur had received the £300 bonus that had been due from the War Office, and Mr Day, the bank manager, had agreed to lend at 9 per cent any further funds the couple required to buy a house. She added that the good news was not to be mentioned in front of Daisy. That afternoon Evelyn told her eldest son, 16-year-old Jules, 'I am going to meet Pa and see a house somewhere near Brent Bridge,' adding that she expected to be able to sign some papers relating to the purchase.

At 8 p.m. that evening Evelyn was having supper with Mrs Orrell. Daisy, who had been working as a cashier at Mrs Hyams' florists and fruiterer's shop at 123 Golders Green Road, arrived home at 8.30 and joined the other two women at the supper table. Mrs Goslett did the washing up and then went out at ten past nine. Jules, who had gone out at seven, returned home at 9.40. Half an hour later he, Daisy and Mrs Orrell were in the dining room when they heard someone arrive and go upstairs.

*Arthur Goslett.*

Jules went up and found Arthur Goslett, wearing his naval uniform, sitting on an easy chair in his bedroom taking his boots off. Goslett asked Jules where his mother was and Jules replied that she was out, adding that he had thought that Evelyn was with him. 'How could she be going to meet me?' said Goslett. 'I had no appointment with her.'

When Goslett came downstairs to the dining room, he sent Jules to a neighbours' house to see if Evelyn was there, but no one had seen her. George Orrell returned home at about five to eleven. Mrs Orrell went to bed and her husband and Arthur Goslett chatted briefly, then retired for the night. Hutchinson arrived home at 11.45 and went straight to bed. There was still no sign of Evelyn.

On Sunday 2 May Constance Hanrahan, the Gosletts' domestic help, arrived at Armitage Mansions at ten to eight. Her first job was to take tea in bed to the residents, but unusually she found Arthur Goslett in the kitchen making himself a cup of tea, saying he had a bad head. He mentioned that Mrs Goslett was not at home and when Constance asked where she was he replied, 'I don't know.' He then returned to bed. Constance was left with the impression that he didn't care if his wife was missing or not. At 8.15 Constance woke Daisy and said, 'Madame has not been home all night.' Daisy said, 'Oh dear, has she not?' The maid then brought tea to Mrs and Mrs Orrell with the same news. Daisy went to tell Goslett that his wife had not returned and he asked her to fetch Jules, which she did. Goslett told Jules to go to his grandmother's flat and see if his mother was there.

Goslett remained in bed, and sent for Mr Orrell. They discussed Evelyn's unaccountable absence, and Orrell said he was surprised that Arthur was not out looking for her. Goslett said, 'Look here old man, what is the good of me getting up and pacing about London for the wife? If she is out of town she will not be back so early on account of the Sunday trains.'

At 9.30 Mrs Binko was surprised by a Sunday morning visit from her grandson, who arrived at her flat asking if his mother was there. When she learned that her daughter had been missing all night, Mrs Binko at once set off for Armitage Mansions. On the way she spoke to PC Charles Potter who was on duty at the crossroads at Golders Green, and asked him to accompany her. They found Goslett still in bed, claiming that he was not well enough to get up and dress and go to the police station to report his wife missing.

At 12.15 that afternoon 54-year-old Reginald Cox of Golders Manor Drive went to the bank of the River Brent with his son to sail a boat and found the body of a woman in the water. It was a secluded spot called Brentmead Place, at the end of Western Avenue, which was then an unbuilt thoroughfare. The police were informed, and two constables were sent to the spot, followed by Dr Shaw, the divisional police surgeon, and Detective Inspector Burgess. Detective Inspector Thomas Duggan arrived at 2 p.m. The woman was lying in the stream partly on her back and right side, her arms at right angles to the body and her head pointing downstream. The body was lifted from the river and laid on the bank where Shaw made his initial examination. The woman was fully clothed in a brown coat and skirt, a green jumper and a felt hat. Her hair was matted together with congealed blood and there were two large and two small scalp wounds. About 8 yards from the stream there was an impression on the ground where the body had lain and more congealed blood. Smears of blood on the grass showed that the victim had been dragged to the bank and rolled into the water. Some tradesmen's bills were found in the pockets and these identified the body as that of as Evelyn Goslett.

Shaw later performed a post-mortem and he found that the wounds had gone as deep as the bone but had not fractured the skull. He believed that she had first been struck with a hard implement which had produced severe concussion and unconsciousness and had then been pushed into the river, where she drowned.

At 3 p.m. Duggan called at Armitage Mansions to see Arthur Goslett. After breaking the news, Duggan asked Goslett to account for his movements since eight o'clock the previous night and gave him the usual caution. Duggan then took down a statement in writing, in which Goslett said he had been in Richmond on business on 1 May and had returned home at ten past ten. Duggan spotted that the trousers Goslett was wearing did not match his jacket and waistcoat, and asked him where the trousers were. Goslett produced the trousers which were damp, and said that the shirt he was then wearing was the same one he had worn the previous day. Burgess found another shirt with a damp sleeve, stains on the cuff that looked like blood and a red smear on the collar. Goslett ridiculed the suggestion that the stains were blood and suggested that the shirt was damp because it had been placed on a chair with

MURDER MYSTERY AT NORTH-WEST LONDON.

*The finding of Mrs Goslett's body.*

the damp trousers. Duggan took possession of the clothes and told Goslett he was going to take him to Golders Green police station where he would be detained pending further enquiries.

'Have you a warrant for that?' asked Goslett.

'No,' said Duggan, 'this is apparently a case of wilful murder and no warrant is necessary.'

'Do you accuse me of the murder, then?' demanded Goslett.

Duggan refused to be drawn. 'You will, as I say, be detained pending further enquiries.' Before they left Goslett called up Daisy and gave her some of his wife's jewellery and some cash for safekeeping.

In the cells at Golders Green police station Goslett had ample time to consider his position. On 4 May he was seen by Superintendent Arthur Fowler Neil and just as Neil was leaving Goslett said, 'Oh, sir I will tell you the truth. I did kill my wife.' Neil cautioned him and Goslett added, 'Yes I want to tell the truth. She forced me to do

*Ex-Superintendent Arthur Fowler Neil, c. 1932.*

it. She kept on at me until I did it. I did it with a tyre lever which you will find in my toolbox in the kitchen behind the pram.'

Goslett made a voluntary statement which was taken down in writing. Refreshing himself from time to time with ginger ale, he began talking at 9.50 p.m. and continued until 2 o'clock the following morning.

Goslett revealed that Daisy was not his sister-in-law but his mistress, whom he had bigamously married under the name of Godfrey, and the child born the previous September was his. His statement continued:

This murder case is entirely my own fault I was forced to do it. On the first occasion when I did not do it I was called a coward, and was threatened by this girl. Her real name is Daisy Holt. This was not the first occasion. She has been running on for about six weeks. On 30 April she wanted me to do it then. My wife was down there but I could not have the heart to do it. I love my wife. I thought the world of her, and this girl tantalized me to kill her. She said there were plenty of places down there by the river. She suggested going down to see the house, stun her and throw her in the river, which I did ... I don't know whether I struck her three or four times, as I had too much whisky down my neck. I did not feel myself drunk but I felt very funny. My limbs gave way. I felt sorry, awfully sorry. I took the body and threw it down in the river.

Goslett said that after taking his wife's jewellery, he returned home and told Daisy he had 'done the job' after which she went to bed with him and stayed with him that night until 4 a.m.

> I told her the best thing was to poison ourselves. She said did I care more for my wife than for her. I said, 'Yes.' I felt I ought to go to the police. She said, 'There will be no clue. Everything will be alright and I will stick to you through thick and thin.' She kissed me. I told her I would never be able to love her. She asked why. I said because she had led me astray.

During the course of this marathon statement the tyre lever was fetched and shown to Goslett who said, 'Yes sir, that is the one.' A handbag and jewellery were also shown to Goslett and he admitted that he had taken them from his wife after he had murdered her.

Goslett then described the murder:

> On Saturday 1 May at 7 a.m. I told my wife to meet me at the Prince Albert [a public house on Golders Green Road] at 9.15 that night to look at a house. When I left home at four o'clock to go to Richmond I put the tyre lever in my pocket. I took it with me for the purpose of killing my wife that night ... I returned by bus to Golders Green. I drank the whisky I had previously taken from home. I spotted my wife waiting for me and said to her 'Come along'. She took my right arm ... We then turned into one of the roads that leads to the place where she was found. I said to her, 'I don't exactly know where it is', referring to the house I was pretending to purchase. As we were walking along she said, 'It is rather a long way' ... I did not know there was a river there until I came up to it. It was Daisy Holt who suggested I should take my wife down to that place and stun her and throw her into the river ... I turned to my wife. I thought it was time to do it. I struck her on the back of the head with the tyre lever. I struck her three or four blows. She was clean gone when she fell ... I took the jewellery from her neck, the pendant and chain, and the earrings from her ears. I looked for a diamond brooch but could not find it ... I kissed her hand with the wedding ring on and said I was sorry and then flung her overboard.

Goslett added that Daisy knew all about what had happened, which was why she came and slept with him that night.

'This is king's evidence that I am giving here,' he added, insisting that those words go into the statement. No suggestion had been made to Goslett that he might evade punishment by blaming another person, but the idea, whether feasible or not, may well have been in his mind.

The statement was read over to Goslett and he signed it. Daisy Holt was brought to the police station for questioning. She said that she knew nothing about the murder and had married Goslett believing him to be a bachelor. She admitted that she had a son, born 4 June 1914, from a previous relationship. Goslett, who had been receiving notes from his wife saying that they couldn't carry on as they had done, had suggested to Daisy that they go away together, but she had said no. Although she had fallen for his persuasive charm, her eyes had been opened and she had begun to feel afraid of him. She thought that he might kill her.

On 5 May, Inspector William Brand went into Goslett's cell at the police station and found him lying on some rugs on the floor. 'Is that other woman still in the building?' asked Goslett, referring to Daisy Holt. When the inspector said she was, Goslett made a new statement:

> This affair is all through her. She alienated my affection from my wife and she has been the instigation of this murder. I am going to have the rope, and I'm going down under. I am speaking the truth, Inspector, believe me. I have been putting it off from day to day for the last six months. I meant doing it a couple of nights before, but my heart failed me. She called me a coward when I saw her afterwards, the same as she has often done. I killed the best woman. I see my mistake. She is a coward. When I returned home on Saturday night I intended to poison myself and I asked her to take poison with me as we were in bed together. She was too frightened and kept pleading excuses that she would like to live for the sake of the child. We spent a wretched night. Believe me, I never intended escaping. I never even troubled to get out of bed and dress. I was in bed when your people came to the door.

Goslett said that he had been born in Cape Town on 15 May 1876, where his father, a native of Kent, ran a livery stable. Arthur had later studied engineering and carpentry at school. When the Boer War broke out he joined the Cape Town Volunteers and later French's Scouts. He had previously worked on aeroplane construction in France. He came to London in 1913 and worked for a firm of builders, then in 1914 passed a test for the construction of aeroplanes at Hendon.

Police enquiries soon revealed a less savoury side to Goslett's past. In 1909 he had been arrested for diamond frauds in Germany and sentenced to four years in prison, which was later reduced to one year and nine months.

On 17 August 1915, while serving with the RNAS at Dover, he had contracted a bigamous marriage with a Miss West-Oram. He made the mistake of marrying her under his real name and was arrested for the offence on 5 October. He appeared at Dover Police Court on the following day, where Evelyn testified, bringing her marriage certificate as evidence. Goslett was bound over at Maidstone Assizes on 25 October and appears not to have served a custodial sentence. When it was learned that he had German associates, he was suspected of spying and was questioned on 20 December 1915, but no charges were made.

A child was born to Miss West-Oram in the following year. Evelyn was presumably a very forgiving person. She took her erring husband back. On 23 January 1916 Goslett was discharged from the RNAS. The highest rank he achieved was that of first class chief petty officer, but for the last three years he had been masquerading in the uniform of an engineer lieutenant of the Royal Navy, something he knew would

*Goslett arriving for his first appearance in court after his arrest.*

enhance his success with women. He had claimed to be both an aircraft constructor and pilot, boasting about his prowess as an aviator, but his real occupation in 1920 was a carpenter employed by a chair manufacturer called Manning. On 4 January 1920, using the name Godfrey, he had bigamously married Ethel Frances Baker, who was expecting his child.

Following his arrest for murder, the police received an anonymous letter revealing that Goslett had proposed marriage to a young woman called Gladys Eldridge and given her a dress ring, which it later transpired he had stolen from Mrs Binko. Fortunately for Gladys, her father had discovered that Goslett was already married and the relationship was broken off and the ring returned. He had also been keeping company with a 31-year-old cook, Miss Ellen Everett.

The inquest on Evelyn Goslett opened at Hendon Town Hall on Wednesday, 5 May 1920. Dr Shaw was shown the tyre lever and said that in his opinion it could have caused Evelyn's injuries. The coroner's officer, Police Constable Leach, then produced Goslett's boots and trousers. The coroner held up the trousers saying that he wanted the jury to remember that the legs were damp. That evening Inspector Duggan formally charged Goslett with the murder of his wife.

On Thursday Goslett appeared at Hendon Police Court. He was represented by his solicitor, Mr Christian Groebel, who could say little on his client's behalf except that he was in ill health, and asked for the £5 found in Goslett's pocket to be returned to him. This was done. 'No doubt the prisoner will require extra nourishment,' commented Inspector Duggan.

On 11 May, Mrs Orrell went to see Goslett in Brixton Prison, taking Leonie with her, and during their conversation he admitted that he had murdered his wife, claiming that he had been drunk when he committed the crime. 'Daisy Holt made me do it,' he said. 'She threatened to give me up for bigamy.'

On 12 May, Daisy was taken to hospital with a suspected miscarriage. Her brother, engineer Herbert Holt, made a statement to the police saying that he had thought from the start that Goslett was a 'crook'. He and his sisters, Ethel and Dorothy, had tried to persuade Daisy to have nothing to do with him but she had been infatuated and ignored their advice. Daisy had seen a telegram, which Goslett must have forged, informing him that he had been promoted to captain. Goslett had tried, unsuccessfully, to borrow £100 from Herbert, and on 14 July last year he had borrowed £3 from Ethel.

When Mrs Binko was questioned at the adjourned inquest on 18 May she admitted that the relations between herself and her son-in-law had not been friendly. 'For every reason I have preferred not knowing him since he brought that woman to his house,' she said.

The relationship that had once existed between Goslett and Daisy had either cooled or been very well concealed after she came to live at Armitage Mansions. Jules, when asked if Daisy was friendly with his stepfather, replied, 'Not that I know of. I very seldom saw them together.'

Groebel objected strongly to Goslett's statements being read out in court, but he was overruled, and the confessions became public knowledge. *The Times* made its opinion of Goslett quite clear by reporting the hearing under the headline 'Blaming a Woman'.

It was not until the final day of the inquest, on 1 June, that Daisy Holt took the stand and was able to give her side of the story. She had been discharged from hospital only two days previously after suffering a miscarriage. Daisy had been born in Edmonton in 1892, the daughter of Richard Holt, an engineer. In 1911 she was living with her widowed mother, Abigail Maria, and her brothers and sister, and working as a factory clerk at an ammunition works. She denied that she had ever incited Goslett to murder his wife or that she knew he had killed her. They had first met in July 1918 and Goslett, who was sporting his naval uniform, told her that his name was Arthur Godfrey, that he was a single man, and that his occupation was testing aeroplanes for firms at Kingston. They started seeing each other and eventually he was introduced to Daisy's family and spent Christmas with them. He proposed marriage to her and a seduction followed. On 5 February 1919, with Daisy two months pregnant, they went through a bigamous marriage. On the certificate he described himself as 'Lieutenant Chief Engineer, Royal Navy'. They lived in furnished rooms at 68 Forest Road, Kew, but sometimes he was absent for the weekend, saying he had to take planes to Dunkirk.

They left the flat in August and Daisy went into a nursing home at Richmond for the birth of the child, but she was only there for a week. Goslett visited her and on the last occasion he took her out to Kew Gardens where he confessed that he was a married man, but assured Daisy that he had no intention of abandoning her. Goslett, who could no longer afford to pay for either the flat or the nursing home, suggested that Daisy should pretend to be the widow of his brother who was killed in the war and come to live with his family. A telegram was sent to Mrs Goslett and that same evening the supposed 'Daisy Goslett' arrived at Armitage Mansions to take up residence. Daisy told the court that she had been unwilling to do this but she was entirely dependent upon Goslett, who, she claimed, had threatened to shoot her if she didn't carry out his instructions. When Mrs Goslett went on holiday, Daisy went to stay with the Mannings, unaware at the time that Mr Manning was Goslett's employer. On 10 September her child was born at the City of London Lying-In Hospital. Daisy returned to the Mannings for two weeks then came back to live with the Gosletts, and obtained employment at Mrs Hyams' florist and fruiterer's shop. Mrs Hyams had known Daisy before her marriage and also knew her as Mrs Godfrey. One day Mrs Manning came into the shop as a customer, and greeted Daisy as Mrs Goslett. The secret was out. Mrs Manning went to Armitage Mansions and told Evelyn what she had discovered and Evelyn challenged Daisy, who refused to say anything until Arthur was present. Arthur Goslett came home to what must have been a stormy atmosphere and was confronted by two very angry women. 'Did you marry me or did you not?' demanded Daisy. He made no reply and Daisy thereupon told Evelyn the whole story.

Arthur retreated to the dining room, leaving Daisy and Evelyn to discuss practicalities. Evelyn, anxious to avoid local gossip and scandal, wanted an amicable agreement. She said that Daisy could remain at Armitage Mansions until arrangements could be made for somewhere for her to go. She advertised for someone to take care of the child and it was agreed that Arthur should pay 10s a week towards its upkeep. Daisy eventually found a couple to look after her daughter for 16s a week, but when she told Goslett his only response was to tell her not to worry him. In the event Arthur only paid her 10s on two occasions.

Daisy was unhappy continuing to live at Armitage Mansions, where she was obliged to share a room with Evelyn's 13-year-old son, and Goslett offered to find her somewhere else to live but he did not. On 26 April Mrs Manning encountered Constance in the street and questioned the maid about Daisy. When Evelyn Goslett realised that her maid knew about Daisy's true status she feared that the secret would become public, and said that something would have to be done. Evelyn told Daisy she would have to leave.

Mr Groebel commenced a hostile cross-examination of Daisy, asking her about the child she had had prior to meeting Goslett. She asked him what that had to do with the case, but he insisted on an answer, telling the coroner that he wanted to attack the witness's credibility. The coroner told Daisy she must answer the question and she replied, 'Yes, and I told the prisoner about it.' Groebel suggested that when living at the flat she had received 10s a week from Arthur, which she denied. Goslett had been listening intently and jumped up and shouted, 'You did, see. Telling lies.' Daisy repudiated the suggestion that she was frequently intimate with Goslett at the flat, saying there had only been one occasion in February or March, and denied that she had ever quarrelled with Goslett or struck him. She was adamant that she had not gone to bed with him on the night of the murder. Daisy agreed that before the police took Arthur away on 2 March he had handed her some articles and kissed her. 'You were very fond of him on that day?' asked Groebel. 'Indeed I was not,' said Daisy. She said that Mrs Goslett was very kind to her and she 'admired her for the way she shielded her husband.'

At the conclusion of the inquest the coroner, Dr Cohen, stated that 'there was not a shadow of evidence against [Daisy Holt].' Arthur was committed for trial.

By the time the trial opened on 21 June, Goslett had made eight statements and six confessions. He was maintaining that he had been drunk at the time of the murder, but everyone who had seen him shortly afterwards testified that as far as they could see he was sober. Goslett's clothing had been examined by Home Office Pathologist Dr Bernard Spilsbury, who had discovered traces of blood on the overcoat and other articles but none on the tunic, trousers or service cap.

Mr Curtis Bennett for the defence tried to prevent the statements made by Goslett on 4 May being used in evidence, claiming that they had not been made voluntarily. The court was told that when Goslett made these statements he had been in custody for two days and had already made two statements in which he said he was innocent. Bennett implied that the prisoner had been intimidated, saying that for six hours before seeing Superintendent Neil, Goslett had been visited every quarter of an hour by an officer at the station.

*Sir Henry Curtis Bennett.*                    *Mr Justice Shearman.*

Sir Richard Muir for the prosecution, anticipating that Goslett would put forward a defence of insanity, pointed out that the motives for the murder were that the prisoner had two women to support and the one he preferred was being sent away. This was 'wicked' but 'intelligible'. Muir believed that there was 'no reason to suspect that the prisoner was not as sane as any of his fellow men.'

Bennett brought Goslett's war record into evidence when he cross-examined Mrs Binko. From the nature of the questions it appears that the main source of information on this subject was his client. Mrs Binko confirmed that Goslett had told her he had served in the Matabele War and the Jameson Raid. 'And in the South African war?' went on Bennett. 'Well, I cannot vouch for every war,' said Mrs Binko. She agreed that Goslett had served in the First World War.

'Do you know that just before the war he had a very severe aeroplane accident?'

'So he said,' replied Mrs Binko, probably one of the last people in court prepared to take Goslett's word for anything.

A police constable was brought to testify that he had visited Goslett every quarter of an hour after he had been lodged in the cells at the police station, but it transpired that these 'visits' only involved observing the prisoner through an aperture, and the constable had not entered the cell. It was claimed that this had been done in accordance with printed instructions. Mr Justice Shearman asked to see a copy of those instructions, which were brought to court on the second day of the trial and showed that ordinary cases were required to be visited every hour and 'drunk' ones every half hour. Why Goslett had been visited every quarter an hour was not clarified, though this may have been advised if it had been felt that he was a suicide risk. Mr Justice Shearman saw no reason why the statement made on 4 May should not be admitted in evidence.

Inspector Duggan testified that nothing had been said to Goslett about the possibility of his evidence being used against another person. As far as he had been able to discover the allegations against Daisy were all in Goslett's imagination.

The defence brought some witnesses to testify as to Goslett's mental stability. Walter Dale was an assistant at an aircraft factory at Cricklewood in 1916 where Goslett had also worked. He found him 'a curious and awkward person to deal with' and 'later I thought he was not right in the head and I took care to avoid him as much as possible.' Dr Frederick Shearman Toogood, described in *The Times* as a 'mental expert', had, until 1919, been superintendent of the Lewisham Infirmary. He was experienced in the supervision of patients with mental disorders, but was not, on his own admission, a specialist; nevertheless, he was willing to state his belief that the prisoner was insane. He had interviewed the prisoner on 17 June, and Goslett had told him that he had been in a plane crash in Germany in 1913, after which he had been unconscious for a day and a half. There were marks on his head consistent with this story. Toogood said that if Goslett had had twenty drinks on the night of the murder as he had claimed, he would have been unfit to judge the nature and quality of any act he committed. However, the only evidence he had that Goslett had been drunk that night was the prisoner's own statement.

The prosecution brought a more convincing witness, Dr Griffith the medical officer of Brixton Prison, who said that he had seen no indications to lead him to suppose that the prisoner was insane.

In his summing up, Mr Justice Shearman made it clear to the jury that they were not considering if the prisoner was eccentric or abnormal, but whether he was mad. He remarked that he had never heard of a murderer who was normal, adding that the jury could dismiss any suggestion that Goslett was obsessed by a crazy notion that Daisy Holt urged him to commit murder.

It took the jury ten minutes to decide on a verdict of guilty and Goslett was sentenced to death. His appeal, on the grounds that the confessions were inadmissible, was dismissed on 12 July. On 26 July he saw Mr Groebel, who could offer him no hope of a reprieve. The condemned man, who was allowed to kiss his daughter farewell, said that he had been ruined through the temptation of money.

Goslett was executed at Pentonville Prison on 27 July. A woman tried unsuccessfully to gain admission to the prison shortly before he was hanged, but she was not Daisy Holt. That morning, Daisy was staying with her brother Herbert. Her sister-in-

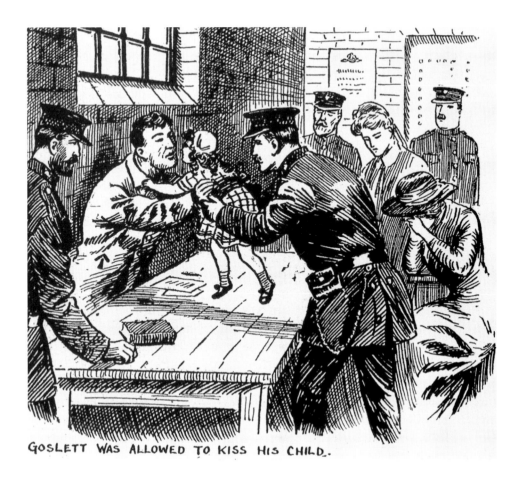

GOSLETT WAS ALLOWED TO KISS HIS CHILD.

*The mystery woman at the prison gate.*

*An artist's impression of the execution of Arthur Goslett.*

law Lena took a cup of tea up to her room, anxious about how Daisy was taking the news. She found Daisy unmoved, saying only that Goslett had got what he deserved.

Not long afterwards the family lost touch with Daisy. She may have married or changed her name, and her subsequent history is unknown.

# 7

# THE RUBBISH DUMP MURDER

*Edgware, 1931*

In 1931, hundreds of tons of rubbish were heaped in an area known as Scratchwood Sidings, alongside the railway line that ran between Mill Hill and Elstree, not far from the Moat Mount golf course. The dump was used by the London Midland & Scottish Railway for the disposal of all refuse collected from stations, goods sheds and coal yards for the London area and serviced the lines going as far north as Bedford and all the way down to Southend. Several times a week rubbish would be brought to the site on trucks and added to the pile. The tip, much like a compost heap, generated its own heat, and in parts was visibly burning. As soon as any new combustible rubbish landed on the tip it began to smoulder. As far as anyone could remember the tip had been burning steadily for over twenty years. On 30 May there was a particularly large consignment, but no work was done in the area during the following two days.

On 1 June, Michael McGlade, a labourer of no fixed abode, arrived in the area looking for work. At about 5.30 that evening he went to Scratchwood Sidings, searching the tip for some wood to make a fire. As he leaned over the smouldering heap to light his pipe he saw something with an unexpected yet oddly familiar shape sticking out of the rubbish. It was a human hand, blackened by the heat, the fingers clenched. Looking closer, he saw, stretched out on the heap, the shape of a man's body. He reported his find at the estate office and the police were called to the spot.

PC William Taylor, who had been on duty on the Watford bypass road, was the first to investigate. Half way up the bank of rubbish he saw a human body lying on its back. Part of the body, from the trunk to the knees and the left arm, were uncovered. He decided to remove the body from the heap, presumably to prevent any further destruction, and found that the right arm and both feet had been completely burned away. The face of the corpse was covered in a piece of sacking. Taylor stayed by his smouldering find until it was taken away. Other items found on the heap near the body were burnt bones, a pair of spectacles and a tobacco tin.

*Scratchwood Sidings, 1931.*

The first message issued to police about the incident stated, 'It would appear that the body is that of the tramp class'. The charred remains were first examined by Dr Church, police divisional surgeon, who was unable to give a cause of death, and the body was taken to Hendon mortuary. There was, at this point, no suggestion of foul play. Superintendent Cornish was informed and visited the scene, and Divisional Detective Inspector Frederick Bennet was assigned the enquiry. A rough description of the dead man was circulated and the coroner ordered a full post-mortem to be carried out.

On the afternoon of 2 June, pathologist Sir Bernard Spilsbury examined the remains at Hendon mortuary. The body was that of a middle-aged man. When he removed the piece of sacking with which the corpse's head was wrapped, the skin of the face came with it. The sacking was heavily bloodstained on the inside. A photograph was taken, but it was obvious that visual identification was going to be difficult. The degree of putrefaction of those parts of the body which had been protected by clothing enabled Spilsbury to estimate that the man had then been dead for two or three days. It did not take long to establish that this was a case of murder. The unknown man had been the victim of a violent attack. Both the jaw and nose were fractured and there was facial bruising that had happened during life. Spilsbury thought that these injuries could have been caused by kicks from a booted foot. The hand had been bruised before death but not in such a position that suggested the man had struck out at anyone. The immediate cause of death was a blow to the left temple, which had been inflicted by a heavy object with a square surface, possibly an axe, which had made a rectangular-shaped fracture of the skull, and injured the brain. The burning had all taken place after death.

Despite the condition of the body, there were a number of clues as to the man's identity, the most important of which was a tattoo on his left forearm of a red heart pierced by a sword. It also appeared that the man had worn a moustache. The clothing suggested that he was a labourer.

It was naturally suspected that the body had arrived at the site in one of the refuse lorries, and the police interviewed platelayer William Ager who supervised the team of twelve men who brought the rubbish to the sidings. He was adamant that since the rubbish was unloaded by means of forks and shovels it was impossible for a body to have been amongst the debris without it being noticed. It was, he said, definitely not there on 30 May.

Detective Inspector Bennet visited the area together with Sergeant Leonard Pickett, of the Edgware CID, whose local knowledge was to prove invaluable. About three quarters of a mile from the sidings, in an area of fields and woodlands dotted with rough bushes and crossed by rural pathways, was a small community of essentially homeless men living a hand-to-mouth semi-criminal existence. They occupied small, roughly constructed shacks, and engaged in casual labouring work. These men were regarded with great suspicion in the area, and were not welcomed at the public houses, as they were 'of a quarrelsome kind'. The community centred around Old Clay Lane (nowadays called Clay Lane), where a stream, a tributary of the Deans brook, provided water for washing and cooking. Nowadays the stream lies underneath the Broadfields Estate. In 1931 Old Clay Lane had not been used as a thoroughfare for many years. It was covered with thick bushes, trees and overgrown hedges, and in places the grass was 4 or 5ft high.

Pickett suggested that the body might be that of one of the shack-dwellers. Bennet, Pickett and Detective Inspector Ernest Andrews made enquiries amongst the little community, asking if any of the men was missing. One of the navvies called James King said that there was a man he hadn't seen in a few days. Some of the itinerants preferred not to go by their real names, and the missing man was nicknamed 'Pigsticker'. King was brought to the police station, where he described Pigsticker as between 5ft 10in and 6ft tall, with a fresh complexion, shaggy dark brown moustache, dark hair balding on top, and of a medium to thin build. When last seen, the missing man had been dressed in a shabby coat with a dark brown-check pattern, a green tweed waistcoat with flaps over the pocket and a velvet back, and the same colour trousers. Shown the fragments of clothing taken from the corpse, he identified them as those worn by Pigsticker.

Later that day another navvy, 59-year-old John Armstrong of Hebburn-on-Tyne, arrived at the police station and made a statement. He had arrived in the region looking for work in late May, and, having no money for even the cheapest lodgings, made his way to what he called 'the Huts'. Initially he stayed with a man called Dick Johnson, known as 'Kingston Dick', then he met up with another man known as 'Moosh', who said that there was room in his hut and Armstrong could stay with him. He moved to Moosh's hut on 25 May and found another man, known

*Clay Lane.*

*A clearing by the side of Clay Lane , the probable site of encampment.*

as 'Tiggy', also staying there. Tiggy had work but Moosh did not, so Armstrong and Moosh went together to sign on at the Hendon labour exchange on 27 May.

On Saturday 30th Armstrong had visited a number of pubs, returning to the hut to sleep at about 10 p.m. Tiggy and Moosh arrived shortly afterwards, and asked 'Are you there?' to which he replied, 'Yes.' They went away, but at about 11 p.m. Armstrong heard noises outside the hut, which he described as about twenty-five loud thuds and a voice saying 'Oh dear'. He recognised the voice as that of Pigsticker, whom he had met previously. Armstrong sat up and looked outside, where he saw Tiggy and Moosh. One of the two – it was too dark to tell which – was striking Pigtsticker with some kind of weapon, possibly a cosh or stick. The incident was taking place just outside the hut in which Pigsticker had been staying. 'I never spoke because I was afraid, knowing Moosh and Tiggy to be determined men,' he told the police.

Things went quiet for a while, and then about twenty minutes later he heard four terrible thuds coming from the same direction as before. He then saw Moosh drop an axe into a pail of water outside the door of the hut where he lay. A few minutes later, at about midnight, Tiggy and Moosh walked past the door in the direction of the siding, Tiggy in front and Moosh carrying the body of a man over his shoulder. Armstrong, still too afraid to do or say anything, remained where he was, wide awake.

About an hour later the two men returned to the hut, and Armstrong pretended that he had been asleep and had just woken up. Tiggy and Moosh lay down to sleep but got up again at 4 a.m. They lit a fire outside, and he heard them going backwards and forwards from Pigsticker's hut. At twenty to seven he got up and found the others sitting by the fire. Moosh started to wash his trilby hat. Unusually, a second fire had been made, and this was being fed with old sacks and what appeared to be pieces of clothing. Moosh kept poking it to make it burn. Tiggy entered the hut and went to bed. Armstrong cooked bacon for the three of them and he and Moosh had breakfast and left Tiggy's in the pan. At about 8.30 Armstrong washed the dishes and put a pail of water and some meat on to cook for dinner. At twenty to twelve Armstrong said he was going to walk to Edgware. Tiggy was still in the hut, but Moosh followed him out into the field and said, 'if anybody asks about the 'Sticker ...?'

'Oh, yes,' said Armstrong, quickly.

'Mum's the word.'

He went on to Edgware and had a pint of beer, no doubt musing over the fact that Moosh knew that he had seen what had happened to Pigsticker and terrified that he was now in danger. He left Edgware at ten past one and went back to the hut, finding the dinner still on the fire but, thankfully, Tiggy and Moosh gone. He packed up his belongings and cleared out.

For the next few nights he slept in an empty house at Colindale. During the daytime he occasionally saw Tiggy and Moosh in the locality. On 2 June someone gave him a newspaper and he read about the man being found dead at a siding tip. He realised that it was Pigsticker and went to Hendon police station to say what he knew.

*The entrance to Clay Lane.*

There were no pictures available of the wanted men, but Armstrong was able to provide detailed descriptions. Moosh was 5ft 7 or 8in tall, of medium build, with a full face, clean shaven, very dark complexion, hair and eyes black, and with the picture of a woman tattooed on his arm. He wore striped cord trousers with a dark blue tweed jacket and a waistcoat with a velvet back and a light trilby hat. Tiggy was about 5ft 4in tall with a thick build, round face, and pointed nose. He too was clean-shaven, with brown hair and a sallow complexion. He dressed in dark blue striped cords, a light grey coat, dark cloth waistcoat and light trilby hat.

Tiggy and Moosh were already known to the police as potential troublemakers, violent men who were quick to take offence, and Sergeant Pickett advised that they owned three ferocious dogs which would bark a warning when anyone approached the hut. Arresting them did not promise to be an easy task, especially as Detective Inspector Bennet had determined that they should be apprehended separately so that each would not know what the other had said.

The police first approached the huts very discreetly at night, and, without alerting the occupants, managed to ascertain that the wanted men were there. Bennet waited until daylight before making his move. He posted officers around the area and placed himself in hiding at the entrance to Old Clay Lane. In the event all was accomplished very smoothly.

At about 7.15 a.m. a man appeared in the lane and Bennet approached him, saying, 'I am a police officer. You answer to the description of a man known as "Moosh".' The man admitted that he was Moosh and Bennet told him he was making enquiries into the death of a man known as Pigsticker and that he would be detained. 'I don't know what you mean,' said Moosh. 'I know nothing about it. All I can say is I saw him when he came home to the hut on Saturday.'

Detective Inspector Andrews and the other officers closed in on the shack, where they found Tiggy outside, sitting by a fire. Asked if he was the man known as Tiggy, he said 'yes.' Andrews cautioned him and said he was taking him to Edgware police station to question him in connection with the death of Pigsticker. Newman said, 'Well, I don't know anything about him being dead. I saw him in a bus in Edgware last Saturday night. That's the last I saw of him.'

Tiggy and Moosh were taken to the station, and surrendered their jackets and hats for examination. Asked to make a statement, Moosh said, 'I don't want to say nothing,' and Tiggy said, 'I ain't got nothing to say.'

Detective Inspector Andrews returned to Old Clay Lane. Searching Tiggy and Moosh's ramshackle hut, he found a bloodstained axe hidden under the floorboards. The distance from their hut to that of Pigsticker's was measured as 140ft. Despite

*Edgware police station, 2009.*

*View across the fields towards the sidings from Clay Lane.*

the overgrown nature of the terrain it was possible to see Pigsticker's hut from Tiggy and Moosh's, confirming that Armstrong could have seen the murder without going outside.

Even days later the signs of a violent conflict were still apparent. Andrews found a great deal of trodden down grass in the area between the two huts, and also a quantity of bloodstained grass which appeared to have been torn off and thrown into a hedge. Close by was a blackthorn briar covered with what looked like blood and human hair.

The only question to which he had no answer was how they had transported the body. The distance from Pigsticker's hut to the rubbish dump was measured at 1,017 yards, and in order to get there the men would have had to cross a field, two fences and two sets of railway lines carrying a dead weight.

A number of people wrote to the police claiming the deceased as a missing husband, father or son, but eventually he was identified as 45-year-old Herbert William Ayres. His brother Edward, a labourer of Watford, read the description of the victim in a newspaper and came to Edgware police station. He identified the body by the moustache, clothing and tattoo. Edwards said that his brother '... was always a man to be roaming round the country and obtained work as a navvy wherever he could ...', but he was not a violent man, had a cheerful nature, and was only quarrelsome 'sometimes when he had beer in him'. Ayres had a number of minor convictions, for drunkenness, stealing a ham, some fowls and some lead, but he had earned his nickname by stealing a pig in Warwick, impaling it on a stick, and cooking it by a watchman's fire.

The two accused men had also given up their real names. Tiggy was 61-year-old Oliver Newman and Moosh was William Shelley, 57. Both had a number of convictions for petty theft.

The two men had not been in custody for long when Shelley said to Sergeant Pickett, 'I will tell you something of what happened.' Pickett cautioned him and took a statement.

William Shelley was born in Ockley, Essex. He had never been to school and was effectively illiterate. He said that he had never had any mental or physical illness or suffered any injury. He had first come to Edgware seven years ago and built a hut in Clay Lane. The hut had burned down and he went away for twelve months, then came back in January 1931 and built another hut, where he had lived ever since. Soon afterwards, Tiggy arrived and the two shared the hut. 'Sticker had come to the area on around 11 or 12 April and put up a hut.' According to Shelley, the dead man was a habitual thief.

'He has been causing trouble ever since he came. Two or three times last week he stole tea and sugar and Tig and I caught him and he ran away. On 28 or 29 May Tig and I talked about it and decided to knock him about for it.' On Saturday 30 May they had missed half a loaf of bread and some bacon and they were sure that Pigsticker had had them as they had tracked his footprints. Between 11.30 p.m. and midnight they were in their hut and when they saw that Pigsticker was outside, they both went out and accused him of stealing. According to Shelley, no sooner

*Newman's shack in Old Clay Lane, 1931.*

THEY CARRIED THE MURDERED MAN TO THE BURNING RUBBISH HEAP

*Tiggy and Moosh dispose of the body.*

was he outside his hut than Pigsticker punched him in the chest and knocked him down. A fight started and Tiggy joined in. 'We had a terrible fight and he was killed,' said Shelley. They had then picked up the dead man, wrapped sacking around his head as it was bleeding, and carried him to the 'shoot' at Scratchwood Sidings and laid him on some rubbish on the bank. 'I did not hit him with anything, only my fist,' said Shelley, 'and Tiggy only used his fists. He [Pigsticker] kicked me when we were fighting.'

Shelley had some refreshment at 8.30 a.m. then said, 'If I could have had my way, you would never have had us. I wanted to put him on a line and let a train hit him. Tiggy would not have it. Still, he's got all he's been asking for, for a long time.' He also explained how they had transported the body. 'We put him in a sack and put a pole though it and carried him across to the tip. It was the hardest job I have ever done.'

At 10 a.m. Newman decided to make a statement to Detective Inspector Bennet. Like Shelley, he claimed to have no history of any kind of illness or injury. He had left school at the age of eight and had been working since he was nine. At 2 a.m. on the Saturday he and Moosh had been at Clay Lane and seen Pigsticker taking tea and sugar out of a box in their hut. 'You've got some bloody cheek,' he observed. At eleven last Saturday night he and Moosh were outside the hut near an opening in the hedge when Pigsticker came though the hedge towards the cabin and they had words with him about stealing their food. Newman, like Shelley, portrayed Pigsticker as the aggressor. According to him, Pigsticker gave him a shove and 'I asked him what game he was up to'. Pigsticker said, 'I will punch you in the jaw' to which Newman replied, 'it will take two to play at the game'. Pigsticker then gave him another shove 'and tormented of me' then 'we had a go for two minutes and I went and laid down.' Pigsticker was then stretched out on the ground motionless, with blood running from his nose. 'I says to Moosh "he must be dead" and Moosh said, "we must take him away".' They wrapped a sack round his head and carried him away and put him on top of the 'dust shoot' and let him roll down. He thought that the ' Sticker had been asking for it a long time.

Both men were then told they would be charged with murder and both said, 'I don't understand.'

There were several witnesses to the ill-will that Shelley and Newman had felt towards Ayres. On the afternoon of 30 May the two men were in the Railway Inn, Station Road, Edgware where they saw Richard Charles Saunders, a labourer, living in a van called 'The Living Van' near Edgwarebury Lane not far from Clay Lane. Something about their manner and expression must have struck him, for he asked, 'You are looking a bit savage. What's up?' Newman replied with words to the effect, 'There will be something the matter if somebody keeps mooching around our place and we lose much more stuff.' He added, 'If they come creeping around many more times somebody will get a "crack".' They made no secret of the fact that they were referring to 'Sticker, and Saunders was relieved to find that they did not suspect him of being the thief. 'He'll find old Tiggy a rum fellow when he starts,' said Newman. 'I haven't got many more years to live, and I don't care a bugger which way it goes.' Saunders decided to leave. He had heard the sound of the fight later that night but had chosen not to investigate.

Another labourer, Fred Cozens, also lived in Edgwarebury Lane, and saw both Newman and Shelley on a bus. Newman had an axe under his coat and nodded in the direction of Pigsticker, who was also on the bus.

Shelley and Newman, described as 'navvies of no fixed abode', were brought before the magistrates at Hendon on 4 June charged with murder.

The two men freely admitted that they had fought with Ayres, but claimed that it was Ayres who had wielded the axe while they had only used their fists. They were held in Brixton Prison pending trial, where both were certified sane.

The trial opened at the Central Criminal Court, Old Bailey on Wednesday 24 June before Mr Justice Rigby Swift. Both prisoners pleaded not guilty. Eustace Fulton and Mr George Buchanan McClure appeared for the prosecution. Fulton and McCure were two of the leading prosecutors of the day. During their careers they acted in most of the important criminal trials to take place in London, and together they would have made a formidable team. Fulton, noted for his firm grasp

*Mr Justice Rigby Swift*

of legal principles, would be appointed Senior Prosecuting Counsel in 1932, and chairman of the County of London Sessions in 1936. McClure, who was less eloquent, was known for his fairness to the accused and was appointed a judge in 1942. The defence counsel had less starry careers; Anthony Jessel defended Newman and Francis Peregrine acted for Shelley.

Home Office analyst, Dr GeraldRoche Lynch, told the court that he had found traces of blood on the men's coats and also on the axe. Sir Bernard Spilsbury's evidence was crucial. He testified that the injuries could not have been caused by fists alone, as the defendants claimed, while the shape of the axe head exactly fitted the fatal wound on the victim's skull.

Counsel for the defence wanted to show that the bruises found on Ayres' left hand were caused when he attacked the defendants, but Spilsbury gave the opinion that the bruises were a result of Ayres defending himself against the blows of the axe. Shelley's counsel later wrote an account of the case in which he said (quoted in Browne and Tullett's biography of Spilsbury), 'We lost, of course, because as every barrister knows, once Sir Bernard has made up his mind, nothing could shake him.'

Mr Justice Rigby Swift was a man who never flinched from stating his own opinions, especially where he felt some aspects of the trial had not been properly conducted. During the trial he expressed his anger at how the defence had made use of the evidence given by Spilsbury at the police court hearings. In a transcript of the evidence, questions put to Spilsbury were made to look as if they were his answers. The judge said:

> In the witness-box counsel listens to him, and if he finds an 'i' not dotted, or a 't' uncrossed, he says, 'This man is saying something different to what he said below.' It happens day after day, and it is painful to see what the art of defending criminals has descended to. I will not tolerate it, and it is a perfect outrage to put that to Sir Bernard Spilsbury and suggest that that is his evidence. It is an outrage. It is shocking!

When Armstrong gave evidence it was revealed that there was more than one thief around. Asked if there was a clock in the hut, he replied, 'No, but there was, and here it is,' producing an alarm clock. Moosh at once recognised it. 'Gor blimey, Tiggy, he's pinched our alarm clock!' he exclaimed.

Newman gave evidence that he and Shelley had not intended to kill Ayres and neither had used a weapon. Shelley supported this story, saying that the fight had begun when Ayres knocked Newman down. He had then helped Newman up off the ground and joined in the fight. When they saw Ayres on the ground they had decided that he was dead. They wrapped the body in a sack and let him lie there for an hour and a half. They eventually decided to put the body on the rubbish dump, which they reached only after crossing some railway lines. The body had been left on top of the dump but they had seen no smoke or fire there at the time.

Mr Jessel submitted to the jury that Ayres' death had been a case of self-defence. The prisoners had denied using an axe, but if the jury decided that an axe had been used then he believed that the verdict should be one of manslaughter. It was a case of what was called in law 'chance medley'. This term refers to a death which arises after a spontaneous and unplanned fight which is so sudden that there can be no malice aforethought and therefore no charge of murder. There had, Jessel maintained, been no intention to kill. Mr Peregrine claimed that both prisoners should be acquitted on the grounds that they had acted in self-defence.

The jury was unconvinced and the two accused were both found guilty of murder. After Mr Justice Swift passed sentence of death on them Shelley said, 'Thank you, Sir. They ought to have done that twenty years ago.' Many people took that to mean that he had other deaths on his conscience, and it was even suggested that the rubbish heap might contain the ashes of former victims.

The prisoners' appeals were turned down on 20 July. Their only hope now lay with an application for a reprieve which was considered by the Home Secretary, labourer's son and former millworker, John Robert Clynes. On 31 July Clynes met with Mr Justice Swift, and said that he had been wondering if the crime had been committed in a drunken brawl and might be regarded as more of a case of manslaughter than murder. Swift immediately stamped on that idea. In his opinion, he said, it was a deliberate murder and the jury had rightly rejected the suggestion of manslaughter made by the defence. He pointed out that the two men had obviously contemplated the murder for some time, and he did not believe that Ayres had attacked them. They had first rendered the man insensible and as he was regaining consciousness some

*Tiggy and Moosh in Pentonville Prison.*

THE CONDEMNED MEN IN CHAPEL.

THEY SHOUTED JOKES THROUGH THE WALL.

*Artist's impression of the double execution.*

THE DOUBLE EXECUTION,

*London Gateway Services (formerly Scratchwood Services), built on the site of Scratchwood Sidings.*

while later they had renewed their attack. It was clear that they had intended to kill him because they had used an axe on the man's head. The Home Office papers record Swift's opinion that it was '... a most ferocious and brutal murder, and he thought that if these two men were not hanged then no murderer should be hanged ... ' Clynes thanked the judge and marked the papers 'no interference'.

Shelley and Newman were hanged at Pentonville Prison on 5 August, the first double execution that had taken place there for several years. At the inquest, the jurors, before delivering their verdict that death was in accordance with the law, asked if they could be permitted to view the bodies. The coroner replied, 'It is permitted by statute. If the majority of the jury desire to view bodies they usually do so. It is late in the day now, as it ought to have been done before the inquest. Now it is out of time. A jury does not have to view a body, and for that, they are generally grateful.'

Scratchwood Sidings was later redeveloped and opened as a motorway service station in 1969.

# 8

# THE WIDOW OF TWICKENHAM

## *Twickenham, 1936*

At 12.35 p.m. on Thursday, 9 July 1936, Constable Thane answered a telephone call at Twickenham police station. The caller, who was male, asked for an officer to be sent to 126 Hampton Road. 'I think the place has been entered. The front door is open.' Thane asked the caller if he had looked inside and there was a pause, then the man said, 'There are some clothes lying about. There may be a body under the clothes.' Thane suggested that the caller enter the house in case the person was alive but he said, 'I am frightened. I will wait for the police.'

Within minutes, a police car was at the house. Sergeant Whapham knocked at the front door but there was no answer. Going around the side he was met by 68-year-old Albert Hadfield, who had made the call from a local post office and then returned to the house. The back door of No. 126 was open. Hadfield said that the owner was a widow, Mrs Laura Mordaunt-Chapman. He took the sergeant to the basement kitchen at the rear of the property, and pointed to a piece of blue paper on the windowsill.

'I came yesterday and left that note, wedged in the window, as I had written two postcards which she had not answered.' Hadfield appeared to be in a very agitated condition, and as he showed Whapham the paper his hand was shaking badly. He said he managed Mrs Mordaunt-Chapman's property. There was a house he wanted to sell for her and that was why he had called and left the note.

The police entered the house and found a pile of newspapers and post in the hallway. Whapham warned Hadfield not to disturb them, but Hadfield ignored him, and picked up two postcards, saying, 'These are the postcards I sent her. I want you to take charge of them as they will show you what I came here today for.'

Hadfield then conducted Whapham upstairs and pointed to a heap of burned blankets and some charred paper lying in the doorway of a bedroom. When Whapham went to examine the heap, Hadfield said, 'You may find a body under there.' The

*Albert Hadfield.*

police officer noticed that a human foot was protruding from the debris. He lifted a blanket which exposed the back and shoulders of a woman. Hadfield exclaimed, 'My God! There it is!'

Whapham commented that there seemed to have been foul play and Hadfield said, 'I don't know. She is a whisky drinker and may have set herself alight.' There was soon a very substantial police presence at the house. Divisional Detective Inspector G. Baker of T division found a bloodstained postcard on the bedroom dressing table. It was undated, and was addressed by Hadfield to Mrs Mordaunt-Chapman. He also found a newspaper lying on the bed dated 6 July and at the bottom of a wardrobe there were ten £1 notes and money orders to the value of £208. The drawers of the dressing table were partly opened. In the kitchen there was a handbag containing £2 in notes and some silver and copper coins. The police examined the premises for signs of an intruder but found no indication of a break-in either through doors or windows. There was no evidence to show that a search had been made for valuables or that anything had been taken.

Detective Inspector G. Haynes also went to the house and Sergeant Whapham handed him the two postcards picked up by Hadfield. Haynes also took charge of the newspapers and letters. One postcard, dated 7 July, was from Hadfield making an

*The finding of
the body.*

appointment to see the deceased at 11.30 a.m. on Wednesday about a prospective tenant. In the card dated 8 July he expressed concerns about the delay in arranging the letting. The newspaper which had been delivered on 6 July had been taken from the letterbox, presumably by the widow, but no post or newspapers had been touched since.

Pathologist Sir Bernard Spilsbury arrived at about 8.30 p.m. and found the victim lying face down and partly on her side in the entrance of the bedroom. A number of stab wounds were visible on her back and neck, and there was a large pool of dried blood on the floor. Close to the top of her head was a pile of burnt material which appeared to be mostly paper. Her right hand was over the pile of paper and had been

*Inspector Cherrill.*

severely burned. There were no residues of petrol or other inflammable liquid that could have been used to start a fire.

The next important arrival at the house was Detective Inspector Cherrill, head of the fingerprint department of New Scotland Yard, who made a thorough search. He particularly noted that the undated postcard on the dressing table had what looked like a thumbprint on it in blood. On examination, he saw that the mark, while not especially distinct, appeared to have been made by a left thumb and there was a white line running through it which suggested that there would be a crease or scar across the thumb that made it.

The house was dirty and in some disorder, however a broken metallic ornament which was one of a pair looked as though it had been recently cleaned, while its partner was covered in dust. The cleaning had not eradicated stains on its base, which later proved to be human blood.

Albert Hadfield made a statement at Twickenham police station. He was the manager of a sweetshop at 14 Nelson Road, Whitton, about a mile from Hampton Road, where he lived with his daughter, Phyllis. He had met Mrs Mordaunt-Chapman about seven years ago when she was giving away apples from her garden. Over the years a friendship and then a business relationship had developed. Mrs Mordaunt-Chapman owned a great many rented properties and had asked Hadfield to find tenants for her. He had been in the habit of calling on her every Monday to attend to her business matters, travelling by bicycle. Hadfield must have been a distinctive figure in the area, an elderly cyclist who habitually wore plus-four breeches and cycling socks.

He had cycled over to see her on 8 July but as she did not answer the door he assumed she was out and left a note saying 'Another wasted journey. If you don't wish to let the house why give me all this trouble for nothing?' and pushed it through the sashes of the kitchen window.

Hadfield told the police that he had returned to the house on 9 July, and going into the back garden, he saw that the paper he had left on Wednesday was still there. He tried the bottom half of the kitchen window and to his surprise it went up. Realising that there was 'something peculiar', he climbed through the window and called out 'are you there?' Getting no reply, he went upstairs and noticed a heap of clothes in the doorway of a bedroom on the right and some burnt material. Realising that something was wrong he left immediately.

Sir Bernard Spilsbury carried out the post-mortem on Friday 10 July. Despite her known fondness for whisky, Mrs Mordaunt-Chapman had not drunk any alcohol for some hours prior to her death. There was a bruise on her head, and Spilsbury believed that the initial assault had been a blow from behind, as a result of which she had lost consciousness and fallen to the floor. She had then been subjected to a frenzied and fatal knife attack. There were forty-six stab wounds on the shoulders, back and neck, all made with a thin-bladed knife about 6 inches long and an inch wide. Her killer had then made an unsuccessful attempt to cover up the crime by lighting a fire. Bed clothing and paper placed around the body were blackened, some of her hair had been singed from her head, and two of her fingers were burned away. He thought that when found she had been dead for at least twenty-four hours and more probably three or four days.

There was no evidence of a struggle, which suggested that Mrs Mordaunt-Chapman had turned her back on someone who she presumably both knew and trusted. She had been wearing only two items of clothing: an outer woollen smock, which may have been worn as a nightdress, and a thin vest underneath. These do seem unusual garments in which to receive a visitor, but the postman later told the police that when he delivered registered letters to the house the lady, who was regarded locally as an eccentric recluse, would answer the door dressed in a nightdress and skirt.

Scotland Yard detectives searched for the weapon, examining every part of the garden and house, and digging up flower beds. They found nothing.

Letters found in the house from Albert Hadfield were all of a business nature. yet they showed that the relationship between him and the widow had been fraught with petty squabbles. Mrs Mordaunt-Chapman often complained about the amount she was asked to pay him for his work, and he objected to her comments as he believed his efforts saved her money. In one letter she had described him as 'the greatest hypocrite it has been my lot to know'. He had been so angry he had replied, 'I return your scurrilous letter, you had better frame it as evidence of the lowness to which a woman can sink when dominated by spleen'. Hadfield attributed her bad

*The home of Mrs Morduant-Chapman.*

*A detective examines the ivy at Mrs Mordaunt-Chapman's home.*

temper to her consumption of whisky. In 1932 he had written her a letter advising her to stop drinking it: '... drink anything but leave that alone it makes [you] too impossible, you were much better when you left it alone, anyhow I cannot put up with your treatment under its influence'.

Mrs Mordaunt-Chapman was born Laura Eliza Davies in Wales in January 1876. She spent her childhood in Usk and had two brothers, Albert and John. In 1905 she married Algernon Mordaunt-Chapman, a property owner twenty-four years her senior. Algernon died in 1922, leaving her twenty rented cottages, two shops and two houses.

After her husband's death she led a quiet, solitary existence. She rarely spoke to neighbours but adored children, to whom she often made small presents of money. Although the house had seven rooms, all furnished, she mainly occupied two basement rooms. Rents were sent by money order delivered to her door. She had few visitors and was nervous about opening the front door to strangers. It was not unusual for her not to be seen for several days at a time. There was a regular arrangement with a public house which delivered a bottle of whisky to her back door every Monday and Thursday. The bottle was left on the doorstep, where money was left in payment. Occasionally, she visited a public house for port and gin. She had last been seen alive in her garden at the back of the house at about 2 p.m. on Monday 6 July.

The police received many letters from local residents about suspicious characters seen in the area, people having been seen with knives, or knives found abandoned nearby. All these leads were followed up but yielded no clues.

Albert Hadfield must have been seen as a strong suspect for the murder of Mrs Mordaunt-Chapman. He was one of the few people she would have let into the house, and there was the potential in their relationship for a quarrel. His behaviour – making no attempt to go to the aid of the widow, and his anxious efforts to establish his reasons for being in the house before the body was found – seemed strange. The police decided to explore the financial side of the relationship between Hadfield and the widow, which they thought might be the key to establishing a motive. Hadfield was questioned at his home on Monday 13 July. He told them that he had once secured an income tax rebate of £400 for Mrs Mordaunt-Chapman and it was agreed that he would receive 10 per cent of that. He had also received small sums of money from her from time to time for writing letters.

Phyllis Hadfield handed over some of her father's clothing for examination. She told Detective Inspector Haynes that her father was a widower, her mother having died in 1929. He went out every Tuesday to collect rent from a house he owned in Clapham, and on Tuesday 7 July he had gone out as usual.

All the articles taken from the house were examined, but although there were specks of blood found on the breeches and mackintosh they were too small for testing, and blood found on Hadfield's gloves was all on the inside.

Whether or not Phyllis was aware of this is unknown, but her mother, Mabel, had not been Hadfield's wife, but his mistress. Albert Hadfield married Julia Eliza Frances Higgins in 1897 and the couple had two children. Their son had died in the First

*Miss Phyllis Hadfield.*

World War and their daughter was a widow who, for the last four years, had been an inmate of Elwell Mental Hospital. In 1936 Julia Hadfield made a statement to the police which was full of bitterness, for she was convinced that Albert had contracted venereal disease before they were married and passed it on to the children. She said that Albert had worked as a commercial clerk but had been discharged in 1901 because of a shortage in the accounts. He was a habitual womaniser and they had separated after four years of marriage. After a brief reconciliation they separated permanently in 1911, after he had formed an attachment to Mabel. Julia told the police that her married life had been unhappy and Albert had been cruel to her: '... when in a violent temper it was a wonder he had not killed me. He appeared at times completely to lose his temper, and on these occasions has not known what he has been doing,' she said.

On 14 July Detective Inspector Baker and Sergeant Bray went to Hadfield's house and found an old pair of cycling breeches and two overcoats. 'What about my breeches?' said Hadfield 'When shall I get them back?' Baker said he would get them back later. Hadfield then said, 'Is there anything on them? If there is, will you tell me about it and I will tell you about the stockings' (i.e. men's golf stockings, normally worn with plus-fours). 'I am not here to bargain with you,' said Baker. 'You can tell me about the stockings if you like.' Hadfield then pointed to a wicker basket which contained the stockings and said, 'They have been washed.

*Albert Hadfield arrives at court in his plus-four suit.*

*Hadfield and his bicycle arrive at court.*

If you had found anything on the breeches it may be creosote. I have got some on this shirt (pointing to three spots on his shirt), I did it when I creosoted a fence.'

This blatant effort to explain away stains on clothing can only have hardened police suspicions.

The crucial piece of evidence against Hadfield was the bloodstained fingerprint on the postcard. When Hadfield's fingerprints were taken, Cherrill noticed that there was a pronounced crease on his left thumb.

The case against Hadfield looked solid – the thumbprint, a possible financial motive and a history of violence. Although the time of death had not been established, Hadfield had said he had not gone to the house on 6 and 7 July, but a witness would come forward who had seen him near the house during those crucial days.

At 7.40 p.m. on Tuesday 21 July Chief Inspector Donaldson saw Hadfield in the approach to Richmond railway station and said, 'I want you to come to Twickenham police station in connection with the murder of Laura Mordaunt-Chapman.' Hadfield accompanied the Chief Inspector to the station, where he was formally cautioned and charged.

Donaldson had already prepared a detailed questionnaire. In particular he wanted to know if Hadfield owed any money to the widow. Hadfield said that he had borrowed £500 from Mrs Mordaunt-Chapman but had paid all the interest up to date. Asked if he had ever offered her marriage he replied, 'I may have done it in a joke, but not seriously.'

On 22 July Hadfield was brought before Brentford Petty Sessions charged with the murder. He was represented by Mr H.N.H. Bransom, a Richmond solicitor, and was remanded for a week. On 25 July Haynes called at Hadfield's home again and Phyllis handed him some of her father's gloves.

The hearing resumed at Brentford Petty Sessions on 29 July, by which time there was considerable local interest in the case and the public section of the court was full. There was a stir in court when Hadfield appeared, white-haired, thin and bespectacled. After proceedings, which lasted only two minutes, Hadfield was again remanded. Crowds waited outside hoping to catch a glimpse of the accused, and the police shut the back door of the court and attempted to smuggle him out. Unfortunately the car was immediately surrounded. Hadfield showed no emotion but kept his head down as he entered the car.

On Tuesday 5 August the case for the prosecution was opened at Brentford police court. Mr L.N. Vincent Evans, solicitor, appeared for the Director of Public Prosecutions and Mr Bransom defended. Phyllis stood at the door of the court and watched her father in the dock though some glass panels.

Evans told the court that witnesses would be brought with evidence which showed that Hadfield had been at Hampton Road on occasions other than those he had mentioned.

A dustman who called at No. 126 Hampton Road would say that he saw a bicycle there on 6 July. A woman would say that on 7 July she saw the figure of a man in the front room of No. 126, and later saw Hadfield come out of the side gate and ride away on his bicycle. On 8 July she saw a man in one of the back rooms and on the same day she saw Hadfield leave the house with his bicycle. A milkman saw someone in the house at 5 a.m. on 9 July.

'If the evidence of these persons is to be believed,' said Evans, 'then the prisoner has not disclosed the whole of the truth to the police.'

Evans concluded that the widow had been struck down by someone who was hidden or someone she knew and was not suspecting. It was not the work of someone who was there for a robbery but 'it would rather appear to be the action of a man who was in a blind rage.'

PC Thane was questioned about Hadfield's call to Twickenham station, and Bransom tried to place a better light on the contact than appeared from the policeman's description. 'Did the defendant say words to the effect "Don't stop to argue, but for heaven's sake send someone along at once"?'

'He did not say that,' said Thane.

'I did!' exclaimed Hadfield.

Bransom, aware that his client had given a poor impression, did his best to counter this.

'When you called on the 13th,' he asked Inspector Haynes, 'were you treated in a perfectly frank, open manner?'

'Quite.'

'Were you offered every facility for searching?'

'Yes.'

When Bransom cross-examined Inspector Baker about his visit on 14 July he said, 'I put it to you that you are mistaken when you say that Hadfield said the stockings had been washed?

'No, sir,' said Baker

'Did he tell you that he had worn them over the whole period?'

'No, sir.'

Baker, like Haynes, agreed that Hadfield had answered his questions in a frank, open manner and without evasion.

The most important evidence was that of Detective Inspector Cherrill, who stated that he had been present when Hadfield's fingerprints were taken. Cherrill was of the opinion that the blood mark on the postcard could have been made by Hadfield's thumb.

That closed the case for the prosecution. Hadfield pleaded not guilty and reserved his defence. He was committed for trial at the Old Bailey.

Things were not looking hopeful for Hadfield, but he was fortunate enough to secure the services of Norman Birkett, the eminent Kings Counsel and future judge who interrupted his holiday to appear for the defence.

The trial opened at the Old Bailey on 23 September before Mr Justice Greaves-Lord. Hadfield entered a plea of not guilty.

The prosecution was conducted by Mr Eustace Fulton and Mr L.A. Byrne, and Birkett was assisted by Mr R.E. Borneman.

Fulton told the jury that it was clear that the murder had not been committed by a thief since money, jewellery, postal orders and treasury notes were found in the bedroom. He suggested that they might conclude that the crime was committed either by a homicidal maniac or by someone who had a quarrel with the victim and made a ferocious attack.

After presenting the facts of the case, Fulton said that specks of blood had been detected on Hadfield's clothing which he thought it only fair to say might have been caused by a cut on the hand. A postcard had been found in the deceased's bedroom with a smear of blood which experts would say was due to the impression of a thumb with a scar across it. The jury would see a photograph of the prisoner's thumb and they would have to ask themselves whether the scar on his thumb was not in the same place as the scar on the thumbprint.

Thomas Arthur Brown, the milkman, said he had delivered milk to the house on 6, 7 and 8 July. On the 9th he had noticed that the milk had not been taken in and, glancing up at the first-floor window, he had seen a figure there. The figure seemed to move away rather quickly. He was unable to say if it was a man or a woman.

Mrs Alice Golledge, who lived next door to Mrs Mordaunt-Chapman, said that she had last seen her neighbour in her garden on Monday 6 July. She saw and heard nothing unusual on Tuesday, Wednesday or Thursday. She had often seen Hadfield in the garden but had not seen him there on the Monday.

*Mr Justice Greaves-Lord.*

*Norman Birkett.*

William Edward Humphreys, a dustman, said that on 6 July he saw a bicycle in the garden of the house. It was similar to Hadfield's, which was produced in court as evidence.

Agnes Elkins lived in Hampton Road in a flat that overlooked the back of Mrs Mordaunt-Chapman's house. On 6 July she saw Mrs Mordaunt-Chapman in her garden. She had seen Hadfield in the garden on many occasions, the last one being on Wednesday 8 July between 12 and 12.30 p.m., so far as she could remember. Her attention had been attracted by the sound of him knocking at Mrs Mordaunt-Chapman's door, after which he had gone away.

She was questioned by the judge, 'you saw him knock rather persistently, and then getting no response from her, turn on his heel and walk through the back gate?'

'Yes.'

The prosecution's star witness was Mrs Florence Dickinson of Bedford Road, Twickenham. She said that on 6 July she was waiting for a bus opposite Mrs Mordaunt-Chapman's house when she heard a noise coming from the direction of the house and saw a man standing in the front room towards the back, looking as though he was cleaning something. She could not see who he was. Returning from her shopping half an hour later she saw a man come out of the side gate of Mrs Mordaunt-Chapman's house. She had identified him possibly as Hadfield. He was wheeling a bicycle and was dressed in plus fours. Counsel remarked that this was the form of dress habitually used by the prisoner.

Fulton asked, 'Can you see that man now?'

The witness looked at Hadfield. 'Yes, that is the man.'

She added that she had seen Hadfield once or twice before outside his shop in Whitton. On 6 July he was wearing knee breeches and had a bicycle. On 8 July, as she was passing the side gate, she saw a man in the back room of the house and about twenty minutes later she saw the same man going out of the iron gate. He had a bicycle with him on that day also. On Thursday 9 July she saw him in Hampton Road with his bicycle.

Cross-examined by Mr Birkett, she said that she had seen Mrs Mordaunt-Chapman many times but had spoken to her only once. It was early on the Friday morning that she had first known that it was suspected there had been a murder.

'I have to challenge a good deal of what you have said,' said Birkett. 'I want to know first of all when it was that you first saw Hadfield, as you say, outside his shop in Whitton.'

'I cannot say definitely. It was Easter or Whitsuntide last year.'

'Did you know him?'

'No.' Mrs Dickinson said she remembered him a year or one and a half years later because his face was so familiar. She saw him again this year for the second time, but could not remember the date.

'I would like to know,' said Birkett, 'because I am to challenge your evidence and do it plainly. When did you see him for the second time this year?'

'It was the same time again, in the holidays of this year.'

'Which holidays?'

'It would be Easter or Whitsuntide. I go out only at those times with my daughter.'

Birkett moved in for the attack. 'With all the multitudes of people that inhabit this world, what reason was there either at Easter or Whitsuntide in 1935 or 1936 to remember a momentary glance at that man?'

'No reason whatever,' she admitted.

'You are telling my Lord and the jury that on those casual meetings you remember his face so well you cannot forget it. Is that right?'

'Yes, sir.'

'When the police asked you about the man you had seen did you describe him by his face or not?'

'No, by his clothes only.'

'Because you could not describe him by his face?'

'Not at that time. I could not until the Thursday.'

'And you remembered him so well. On the Tuesday morning you had no reason at all to suspect that there was going to be a tragedy at the house, had you?'

'No, sir.'

Birkett went on to question her about the figure she had seen at the window and she admitted that she had only glanced at it. She was certain that it was a man and he appeared to be cleaning something, but she did not know who it was.

In reply to further questioning Mrs Dickinson said that on the same day, about three quarters of an hour later, she happened to be passing the house and saw Hadfield. The following day she saw a figure at another window but could not identify the figure. Coming back that day she had seen Hadfield.

'If it was suggested to you,' said Birkett, 'that the prisoner was miles away on any of those dates you mention that you say you saw him, would that shake you?'

'No, sir.'

She added that the figure she had seen at the window was using a small black cloth to do the cleaning.

'You must have had a pretty long glance to see all that?' said Birkett incredulously.

'It was most distinct,' she said.

Despite this she was unable to say what it was that was being cleaned.

'Are you certain it was this man?'

'It was the clothes I was certain about.'

'Did you look at his face?'

'No, I just glanced at him.' Mrs Dickinson described the bicycle with a black bag at the back. She was shown the prisoner's bicycle on which there was a black bag and identified it as the one she had seen. She eventually admitted that she was only able to identify Hadfield by his clothes.

Cherrill gave evidence about the fingerprint, but he confirmed that the impression was too blurred to allow a definite identification.

When the case for the prosecution closed, Birkett submitted that there was no evidence to show that Hadfield had any complicity in the crime and there was no case to go to the jury. Mr Justice Greaves-Lord disagreed – he ruled that there was evidence to go to the jury and case for the defence was opened.

Hadfield took the stand. He said he had known Mrs Mordaunt-Chapman for seven or eight years and assisted her in the management of her property.

'You are wearing a plus-four suit with golf stockings and shoes,' said Birkett. 'That was the kind of dress you were accustomed to wearing?'

'Yes, for many years.'

Hadfield told the court that Mrs Mordaunt-Chapman always insisted on her rents being sent by money orders. She would not open the door unless she knew the time a person was coming because there were so many undesirable people knocking at the door. In reply to Birkett he asserted that he did not go to her house on the Sunday, Monday or Tuesday. On Wednesday 8 July he did not go out until after 11 a.m. Birkett said, 'Mrs Dickinson has said that she saw you coming out of the gate of Mrs Chapman's house with your bicycle at 10 a.m. Is there any truth in that?'

'Certainly not; I was at home.'

'You know Mrs Dickinson has said that she saw you between 2.30 and 3 that afternoon?'

'It is impossible; I was at home.'

Hadfield said that on the Thursday 'something told him' to go to Mrs Mordaunt-Chapman's house. When he arrived there he saw the note which he had previously left still there, and, realising there was 'something peculiar', he went in.

Questioned about the postcard with the thumb mark on it he said he could not say how the mark got on the card.

Mr Birkett put a direct question to his client, asking if he had anything whatsoever to do with the death of Mrs Mordaunt-Chapman. Hadfield replied emphatically, 'Nothing whatever.'

Before any further witnesses for the defence could be called, Mr Justice Greaves-Lord addressed Mr Fulton: 'Is it safe upon this evidence to put anyone on jeopardy?'

'My view is that it is not safe,' said Fulton. 'It would be very dangerous in my view on such evidence as this.'

Greaves-Lord addressed the jury. 'You have heard Hadfield's evidence and what counsel for the prosecution has said. If you are of the same opinion, there is an end of the matter.' After a short consultation the jury found Hadfield not guilty and he was at once discharged.

Phyllis had been sitting outside in the corridor with her fiancé, band sergeant William Williams. They were soon joined by a crowd of men and women who offered their congratulations. 'I always knew I was no murderer,' said Hadfield. 'This trial has established my innocence. It is up to the police to find the real murderer of Mrs Mordaunt-Chapman. They should have done that before.'

Soon afterwards Hadfield and his daughter drove away in a taxi. Birkett took off his wig and gown. 'Perhaps I can go back to my holiday now,' he said. Soon afterwards he was seen running happily down the steps of the Old Bailey. Unusually, he later received a letter of thanks from his client.

*Phyllis May Hadfield arrives at court with her fiancé.*

'Please allow me the privilege of expressing my gratitude for your magnificent defence against the charge of that horrible crime,' wrote Hadfield, 'also for your generosity in meeting my very limited resources.'

Hadfield naturally felt aggrieved at being charged with murder and wrote several letters to the Home Office complaining about the way he had been treated and demanding to know what was being done to apprehend the murderer. He even accused a neighbour of the crime, although the man had long ago been questioned and cleared. A note in the police file dated April 1937 about Hadfield's accusations reads '... he might well be given some friendly advice on the subject of leaving well alone and getting on with his business'.

Phyllis and William were married in 1938. The murder of Mrs Mordaunt-Chapman remains unsolved.

# 9

# THE MAN WITH A SCAR

*Ruislip, 1939*

Sidney George Paul and his Belgian wife Claire appeared to be a devoted couple. Sidney was born in Battersea on 22 July 1892. At the age of 18 he went to Australia where he later joined the Army. He was serving in Belgium in 1918 when he met attractive dark-haired Claire Maroye, and they were married on 21 July 1920. Claire's father, Leon, had been a brewer, but during the war the copper equipment had been seized and he had turned to cultivating his land. Sidney Paul spent some time working for a Belgian company in the Congo, then returned to Belgium, bought land from his father-in-law, and undertook a number of business ventures, all of which failed. Leon Maroye died in February 1937.

In November 1937 Sidney Paul was back in England and called on his brother, Harry. Sidney looked unwell, and said he had had a lung removed. He told Harry that he had had to sell up his business in Belgium after a run of bad luck and was looking for business opportunities in England. He also paid a visit to his married sister, Mrs Frances Goadby, who found him so changed that at first she hardly recognised him. She thought he was under a great deal of stress.

Three months later Harry saw Sidney again, and found his brother looking rather better. Sidney said he was going to be an agent for a sack and bag manufacturer and was planning to bring his family to England.

The Pauls came to live in London in February 1938, together with their three daughters, 16-year-old Nancy, Mary (14) and Clairette (12) and their 7-year-old son, Leon. They bought a house at 19 Rosebury Vale, Ruislip, paying a deposit of £50. In October 1938 Claire Paul was six months pregnant with her fifth child.

The family's efforts to make a new life proved to be fraught with problems. On 9 May a fire broke out at their home in the early hours of the morning, and only prompt action by neighbours who put a ladder up against the wall of the house enabled them to escape. The family stayed with Mr and Mrs Draisey at No. 22 until the repairs to their house were completed. Two weeks later there was another less serious fire. Nancy was treated for nerves by the family doctor, Dr Gerald McCarthy

*Mrs Claire Paul.*

*Rosebury Vale.*

of Park Way, and it was decided to send the two eldest girls to a convent school in Belgium. Sidney was also suffering badly from shock. Neighbour Arthur Jones, at No. 21, was to comment that after the fire Paul had not been the same man. Paul had explained his nervous disposition by claiming that he had been in an air crash while serving in the RAF.

When Harry next saw them in July, Paul said that he was earning £10 a week marketing goods, but he also confided that he had heart trouble and his doctor had told him to make his will. In August, Paul approached an estate agent saying he wanted to sell the house as they were 'going north'. On 7 September he went to his doctor with a badly cut wrist, explaining that he had accidentally put his hand through a window. Three days later, Sidney confessed to his brother that he had not been working. He looked ill and said he had been having injections for his 'heart trouble'.

In late September, Paul told Arthur Jones that there had been an attempted burglary at his house. He said he had found some silver and a clock tied up in a table cloth on the dining room floor, and thought that someone had got in through the conservatory door. 'I did not tell Mr Paul so but I formed the opinion that he had imagined the occurrence,' said Jones, later. 'In fact my knowledge of him gave me the impression that he was a very imaginative person ...' Arthur Jones was one of Sidney's few acquaintances who had spotted his tendency to embellish the truth with a touch of drama, and conceal anything he felt unpalatable. Sidney's claim to have been in the RAF was undoubtedly fantasy, and his doctor's records made no mention of either a lung operation or heart injections.

On the morning of Sunday 16 October Clairette and Leon left home between 7.30 and 7.45 to go to church, leaving their parents alone in the house. Shortly after 8 a.m. Sidney Paul hammered loudly on the front door of No. 20, which was directly opposite.

A police sergeant lodged there, but he was out on duty. The landlady, Mrs Woolley, looked out of the window and saw Paul standing outside, his face streaming with blood. 'Come quickly!' he said. 'There is a man in my house!' Mrs Woolley quickly alerted Mr Broadhurst at No. 18. The neighbours descended on the Pauls' home and found a shocking sight. At the back of the house was a veranda with a glass roof forming what was referred to as a 'summer house' or 'sun room'. Claire Paul was lying face down on the floor of the veranda. She was unconscious and had suffered severe head wounds. Paul was crouching beside her. 'There was a terrible man in the house with a blue coat on,' he said.

'Which way did the man go?' asked Broadhurst.

'I don't know,' exclaimed Paul, 'he may be in the house yet, and I have £150 upstairs in the wardrobe!' If Broadhurst thought this was a curious thing to be concerned about as the man cradled the bloody head of his wife, he did not comment.

William Cooper, who was Jones' son-in-law and lived with his wife at No. 21, went to fetch a doctor and returned with Dr McCarthy, who did what he could for

*The sun room where the murder took place.*

the injured couple. Constables Carlin and Wilkins were the first policemen on the scene and found Paul in a highly agitated state, exclaiming, 'There he is again! He will get me if you don't watch him!' Comforted by neighbours, Sidney wept, 'What will become of the children? Poor little dear, she didn't deserve that.'

Soon afterwards an ambulance removed Claire Paul to Hillingdon Hospital where she lay unconscious in a critical condition. Sidney asked PC Wilkins if his wife was all right and said, 'Don't tell me a fairy story. I have been a soldier and can stand the shock.'

Paul told the police that he and his wife had been attacked by a tall man who had come to rob them. His wife usually kept money in a black wallet in the wardrobe. A careful search was made of the house, but there was no sign of the intruder. Paul showed PC Carlin a double wardrobe in the front bedroom which was partly open. The contents of the wardrobe were tidy except for some folded sheets which had been slightly disturbed, and there were the marks of a sharp implement on the door with the lock. Paul said, 'The money should be in a black leather wallet behind those sheets', indicating the second shelf from the top. He felt along the shelf and shook his head.

The police asked Mrs Draisey to look after the two children, who were on their way back from mass, and she intercepted them and took them to her home.

At 9.30 Paul was seen by police divisional surgeon Wilfrid Max Wilson and afterwards made his first detailed statement to Detective W. Knott. He said that he had been upstairs in the WC while his wife was downstairs mopping the floor of the veranda. He had heard her voice but had assumed she was talking to the cat. He then heard a noise like someone walking about in the bedroom and opening the wardrobe door. When he went to investigate there was no one in the room, but shortly afterwards he heard his wife screaming and rushed downstairs. He found Claire lying on the floor, and was faced with an intruder who knocked him to the ground. 'I got up,' he said, 'and saw a man, clean shaven, with black hair, a black cap, and a blue jacket, rubber boots, and rubber gloves. He had a scar on his right cheek, white and vivid. I closed with him, but he got away. I pulled a button off his coat.' Paul handed the policeman a round dark button. The button was of a distinctive design in that it had no vertical holes or shank, but a transverse slot at the back where a needle could be inserted. Attached to it was a small piece of dark blue linen thread. Paul explained his head injuries by saying that the intruder had struck him on the head and slammed him against the garage wall, temporarily stunning him. A description of the wanted man was sent to all police cars.

Divisional Detective Inspector Charles Ferrier made a thorough search of the house, and took samples of hair and blood at the scene. There was a blood-soaked pillow and matted hair on the veranda, smears of blood on the door jamb, and blood and hair in the sink, which was later found to have been left by Dr McCarthy. Outside the veranda there was an overturned bucket containing some coloured liquid and with blood spots inside, and behind a piece of board against a wall next to the veranda door was an axe with a floor cloth wrapped around its head. There was reddish staining on the shaft, and the cloth and the axe were wet. On the wall of the garage were bloodstained patches. He could find no obvious sign that there had been a break-in.

As it appeared that the intruder could only have entered via the garden, Knott examined a gap in the hedge at the bottom of the garden, which backed onto a sports ground, but found it was effectively closed by barbed wire. Sub-divisional Inspector Emery examined the area near the hedge, where the ground was wet, but found no footprints.

*The police enter the Pauls' villa on 16 October.*

*A police photographer leaves the Pauls' house as an officer keeps guard on 16 October.*

Chief Inspector Cherrill of the fingerprint division made an exhaustive search of the house and took away the wardrobe door.

At Hillingdon County Hospital Claire Paul was attended by Dr Eric Boxall Jackson. She had multiple injuries to her scalp which went right down to the bone, and a fractured skull. Jackson believed that the wounds had been made with a blunt instrument. There was also a deep lacerated wound on the back of her right hand and an abrasion on her right forearm.

Sidney Paul was admitted to the same hospital at 10.35. Jackson found six incised wounds on the patient's scalp, most of which were half an inch to an inch long. There was also one superficial wound an inch and a half long with some bruising at the middle. Jackson thought that Paul ought to be detained but he refused to stay. Inspector Ferrier saw Paul at the hospital and once his injuries were dressed, took him to Ruislip police station where he made a long statement.

*Sidney Paul, pictured leaving the house on 18 October.*

Paul admitted that he had not had any employment since coming to England, and the family had been living off the money he had brought from Belgium. The death of his wife's father had not made them wealthy, as many people had supposed, since Leon Maroye had left only one acre of land to be divided amongst seven children. Sidney said that his wife was 'peculiar with money; she seemed to hide it all over the place' and there had been £150 in a wallet in the wardrobe. That morning he had been attacked by a scarred man wielding a heavy stick, and after giving the alarm he had returned and knelt by his wife. She had gasped out 'Papa, Papa, his crucifix' in French, referring to her father's crucifix hanging on the wall. This was placed in her hand.

At 6.15 the same day, Claire Paul died in hospital without regaining consciousness. Sidney returned home and his brother Harry came to look after him. Sidney told Harry that the man who had attacked him was not dressed as an Englishman but looked like an itinerant onion-seller. Harry found his brother suffering abrupt mood-swings. One moment he would be 'wound up and full of energy' and then he would appear 'morose'. 'He had a wild look about him,' said Harry later, adding that sometimes Sidney didn't appear to understand simple things and there were periods for which his mind was a complete blank. He also claimed that he was engaged in secret service work for which he had a specially numbered passport. The children remained with Mrs Draisey but their father was permitted to visit them.

As the police investigation continued, Sidney Paul's story rapidly fell apart. The residents of Rosebury Vale, and the newsboys and delivery men who frequented the area were interviewed, but no one had seen anyone matching the description of the man with the scar.

When the wardrobe was examined it was found that the mark on the edge of the door was, when the doors were closed, completely covered by the flush beading from the other door, which meant that the mark had been made when the door was open. The wardrobe key, which was in the lock, was unmarked.

Detective Inspector Harold Cripps found a box containing five small buttons in a drawer in the kitchenette. While smaller than the button which Paul said he had torn from the intruder's coat, they were of identical design. One of them had a piece of dark blue linen thread attached to it, the same as that in the large button.

Doctors Wilson and Jackson both concluded that the clean shallow cuts on Paul's head had been caused by a sharp instrument such as a razor blade. There was a slight bruise which could not have been enough to stun him as he claimed. It was thought that he had cut himself, and then smeared his blood on the wall.

It was not hard to find a motive for the murder. Unknown to their relatives and friends, and probably unknown to Claire, the Paul family was in dire financial difficulties.

On 18 February Sidney had borrowed £150 from his sister, Frances, saying that he only needed the money for a few weeks to get some goods out of bond for his sack and bag business. The weeks went by and despite numerous promises the money was not repaid. In August Frances went to see Sidney and came away with an IOU. At the beginning of September Frances' husband, Albert, went to see Sidney who asked him to put off payment a little longer. Claire was at home at the time and, realising that there was a problem, she went round to see the Goadbys that same evening. When they told her about the loan to her husband it was obvious that she knew nothing about it. The next week she gave Albert £10 and said she would repay the loan in instalments. On 19 September Paul handed over a cheque for £150. There was 7s 2d in his account at the time, and the cheque bounced.

On 27 September Albert called on the Pauls to make a definite arrangement for repayment of the loan, and they said they would pay him £8 a week. Nothing further had been paid, and a few days later Sidney borrowed an additional £2 from Albert.

Sidney, now desperate for money, went to Father Edward Stanley Sutton, a Roman Catholic priest of Ruislip, who had known the family since their arrival in England,

and asked him for a loan of £25. Sidney claimed he would be able to repay the money on 15 October when 'his usual cheque' arrived. Sutton said he didn't have the money to lend.

On 11 October Frances went to see the Pauls about the money, and Claire confessed that Sidney had said he had lost his money on horse racing. Frances was sure that her brother was mentally unbalanced. He sometimes said odd things such as claiming he was having injections in his leg for his 'funny old head'. The children had also noticed that something was wrong, telling Frances that their father was 'funny sometimes' and pointing to their heads.

Earlier that year Sidney had asked his nephew, 30-year-old Stanley Goadby, if he would work for him in his sack and bag business. Stanley agreed and worked hard getting orders for goods, receiving small amounts of commission, but the orders were never fulfilled. Sidney then opened an account with a bookmaker with a limit of £25, and asked Stanley to place wagers for him, saying he would pay him commission out of winnings. Stanley was instructed to back racing tipster Bouverie's selection in the *Daily Mirror*. At the time of Claire's death Stanley had last seen his uncle in July, when he said things were not too good. Sidney had then claimed to be receiving an income of £10 a week from a glass manufacturers, but, said Stanley, 'I did not believe a word of this as he was always vague about his affairs in general.'

Bouverie did not help Sidney Paul out of his financial troubles. The £25 was spent, and on 11 October a county court warrant was issued for repayment, which, with legal expenses, came to over £30. Paul went to see an officer of the court and promised to pay the money. He was in arrears with his mortgage, insurances, school fees, utility charges, and medical bills, and his bank account was overdrawn by 4*d*.

On 19 October, Inspector Ferrier arrested Sidney Paul and charged him with the murder of his wife. 'I didn't do it! I didn't do it!' Paul exclaimed. 'It's not right. It can't be right.' Later he added, 'I don't know why you say it. You are probably saying this for a joke. We have lived together eighteen years.'

When Paul appeared at Uxbridge Police Court on 20 October, the clerk read out the charge and had reached the words 'you wilfully murdered Claire Paul' when Paul interrupted 'Oh no!' Thereafter he made repeated denials from the dock. He was remanded for eight days, and as he left the dock two officers had to support him under his arms as he went down the stairs to the cells.

At Uxbridge Police Court on 1 November, Mr L.N. Vincent Evans appeared for the director of public prosecutions and Paul was represented by Mr R.R.A. Johnson. Evans submitted that Paul's statements were false and there was never an intruder in the house. He also suggested that there was no cash in the wardrobe, as the family was in need of money at the time.

Johnson did his best, getting Father Sutton to agree that he would describe the Pauls as a happy and devoted family. Commenting on the police questioning of Paul, Johnson tried to elicit sympathy for his client, saying, 'I think the poor man was nearly badgered to death.'

*Uxbridge Police Court, 2009.*

When Dr Wilson told the court that the wounds on Paul's head could have been self-inflicted, Johnson did his best to demonstrate that the injuries were more serious than Wilson stated. 'Are you sure,' asked Johnson, 'that there were no other injuries than the clear incised wounds and the bruise?'

'I saw no others,' said Wilson.

Johnson asked him to walk over to the dock, where Paul lowered his head for Wilson to examine. When Wilson returned to the witness box Johnson asked, 'Will you agree now that there are marks on the head which are abrasions?'

'Yes, there are small marks,' admitted Wilson.

The two most important witnesses in the case were the Pauls' next-door neighbours, composer William George James Cooper and his wife Myvanwy Grace who lived at No. 21 Rosebury Vale, with Myvanwy's father, Arthur Jones. The Coopers' bedroom window afforded a view through the glass roof of the Pauls' summer house, and on the morning of the murder, both the Coopers had been alerted by the noise and looked out, yet they had seen slightly different things, and on the face of it, William's testimony appeared to support the prosecution and his wife's the defence.

Myvanwy Cooper told the court that at 8 a.m. on 16 October, she had heard Mrs Paul call out something in a state of alarm. The words sounded something like 'Mercy! Please! Please!' Getting out of bed she looked out of the window and down into her neighbours' summer house, but seeing nothing she went back to bed. Soon afterwards she heard some groaning, and looked again. This time she saw Sidney Paul in a sitting position on the floor near the door of the summer house. He had his hands up and was pushing someone away from him. The other person was in a stooping position and had their hands on his shoulders, but Mrs Cooper could not say if it was a man or a woman. All she could recall was that the person was in dark clothes, and Sidney's head was covered in blood. She at once called her husband and he, too, looked out of the window.

William Cooper said that he had heard what he described as a few sharp screams in a woman's voice from the direction of the Pauls' house. Looking through the window he saw what he thought was the figure of a woman with her back to him, in a stooping position near the summer house door. He didn't recognise her as Mrs Paul as all he could see was the lower part of the body but he saw that she was wearing a dark skirt, which was how Claire was dressed that day. He didn't take any more notice of the incident, 'as I thought the woman screamed owing to mice, and I moved away'. The noises from next door continued, however. This time it sounded as if someone was 'shuffling about' and Cooper went back to the window for another look. He now couldn't see the woman but he saw Sidney Paul in the corner of the summer house near the door. 'He leaned forward, stooped, and picked something up

*Mrs Myvanwy Grace Cooper.*        *Mr William Cooper.*

from the floor, and made a half turn to the right, bringing him facing the kitchenette door. He then made some striking motions with his hands at something on the floor. I turned away from the window as I did not think it was anything that concerned me.' Cooper said he had assumed that Sidney was trying to hit a mouse on the floor.

Soon afterwards the Coopers heard Sidney calling out for help, and, looking out of the window, William saw his neighbour standing in the garden with blood streaming from his head. Cooper and his father-in-law at once went down to see what they could do and found Sidney half sitting on the floor beside his badly injured wife. 'Oh, Mr Cooper, there is a terrible man in my house with a blue coat on,' were Sidney's first words.

Pathologist Sir Bernard Spilsbury testified that Mrs Paul had suffered at least fifteen blows to the head. He agreed that all the serious injuries could have been caused by the cutting edge of the axe found in the Pauls' house.

Further damning evidence was supplied by Home Office analyst Dr Gerald Roche Lynch who said that the axe appeared to have been washed. The condition of a floor cloth was consistent with it having been used to clean a bloodstained object.

The trial opened on Monday 28 November at the Central Criminal Court, Old Bailey before Mr Justice Asquith. Sidney Paul pleaded not guilty. The prosecution was led by Mr G.B. McClure and Mr Christmas Humphreys, and Paul was represented by Mr J.F. Eastwood KC MP and Mr E.J.P. Cussen.

McClure told the court that the motive for the murder was undoubtedly financial. 'Sometimes a banking account is a very revealing thing,' he said. The loan of £150 had gone in but by the time the next item was paid in, this money had gone. The next item was a receipt of £290 from an insurance company in respect of the fire. It was, he added, only right to mention that there had been no insurance on Claire Paul from which her husband might have benefited.

In view of Sidney's claim that his wife had asked for a crucifix as she had lain injured, McClure asked Spilsbury if a person with the injuries suffered by Mrs Paul could have spoken. 'It would have been quite impossible,' said Spilsbury.

Mr Eastwood asked Ferrier if it was true that Mr Lanfear, the keeper of the sports ground at the back of Paul's house, had said he saw footmarks leading from a gap at the end of Paul's garden to the sports ground. 'If his statement were true, that there were fresh footmarks at nine o'clock, it is a matter of some importance to the defence,' Ferrier agreed.

Eastwood told the jury that the Pauls were 'as happy a couple as they could wish to find.' He maintained that there was no motive for the 'brutal cold-blooded murder'. The only motive that had been suggested was that Paul was hard up and had come to the breaking point, but Eastwood said that there was every hope of the Pauls selling their house for £1,100, of which they would receive £300.

Sidney Paul went into the witness box, where his examination was to take two and half hours. That morning, he told the court, after his children had gone to mass, he went out for some cigarettes and when he came back he went upstairs. He heard a sound which he thought was Mrs Paul talking to the cat. 'I heard the doors of our wardrobe opening. I could hear that because the doors squeak. Then I heard a shout.' He went downstairs and found his wife lying on the floor in a 'frightful state'. He lifted her head and asked her what was wrong but she did not answer. As he went towards the garage he saw a man standing there. He got 'a crack on his head'. There was a struggle in which he received cuts and bruises to his head. He thought the man had hit him with a small stick. During the struggle his head came into contact with the garage wall.

Eastwood queried part of Paul's earlier statement. 'Are you certain your wife said in French to you "Papa, Papa, his crucifix"?'

'It seemed to me that she said that,' said Paul. He went on to say that he had found a button in his hand with his handkerchief when he returned from the police sergeant's house and had assumed it came from the man who had attacked him.

Paul said that he had no objection to his wife having another child, and no motive to injure her. He said he had told the whole truth from the start.

McClure decided to give Paul the opportunity to confess. He first established that Paul had been unwell in September and October suffering from insomnia. 'I am not asking you questions suggesting that this was a brutal murder. I am going to suggest to you and to the jury that this was a merciful murder. I want you to understand that.'

Paul did not take the bait. He said that in August he had gone to the British Legion and asked if they could find him employment. He had brought £380 to England and given it to his wife for expenses. He had been living on his capital.

McClure asked how much money Claire had had in the wardrobe in May.

'£60 and £240 in a black wallet.'

'Why have you not said before that you had £300?' asked McClure.

'No one has ever asked me,' replied Paul.

Paul confirmed that in October his wife had £150 in the wallet upstairs and in response to a question by the judge claimed that she had known he had borrowed £150 from his sister in February.

When Paul mentioned the September burglary at the house, McClure, who was surely suggesting that two fires and two burglaries in just over five months was somewhat farfetched, asked, 'Are you sure it was a burglary or your imagination?'

'I know it was a burglary,' said Paul. He thought it was 'one of those French chaps who sell onions.'

McClure asked him how such a man would know that there was £150 in the wardrobe and Paul replied, 'I know that when they used to come round my wife used to make tea and have conversation with them in French.'

'I suggest that all this story is pure imagination and that you have invented it,' said McClure.

'Not at all,' said Paul, but, unable to restrain himself from adding unnecessary embellishments to an already unlikely story, he now mentioned for the first time that the rubber gloves worn by his assailant were pink, something which contradicted what Mrs Cooper had seen.

There was one medical witness for the defence, Dr M.J. Arnott, who said he had examined Paul's head a month after the tragedy and found six clear scars. Under three of them there was a definite impression on the bone of the skull showing that a certain amount of violence had been used. In his view it was possible but difficult to imagine that the wounds were self-inflicted.

An estate agent, Mr W. Rainsbach, confirmed that Paul had been negotiating with him for the sale of the house for £1,100.

There were only two witnesses who supported Paul's version of events; Mrs Cooper, who had seen the unknown person in dark clothes who Paul had pushed away, and groundsman Cecil Lanfear, who lived in a pavilion of the RAF sports ground behind the garden of the Paul's house. Lanfear described the footmarks he had seen leading across the ground to a gap in the hedge in the Pauls' garden, but admitted in cross-examination that there had been a rugby football match on the grounds on the afternoon of the day before the crime.

Mr Eastwood made his final address to the jury. He did not believe there was sufficient motive for a devoted husband to kill his wife. He said that Paul had not yet received the bill for his children's education and there was no threat to cut off water or light. Could the jury believe that his debts had caused him to reach breaking point? He attached especial importance to the evidence of Mrs Cooper.

Mr Asquith summed up. He said the jury might wonder why, if there was £150 in the wardrobe, none of it had been used to meet the family's pressing financial difficulties. Money worries and insomnia might, he thought, drive someone to 'extreme courses'. He described the evidence for the prosecution as 'very formidable indeed' but then there was the evidence of Mrs Cooper. If the jury thought she did see a third person they might well feel it was very dangerous to convict. If they thought she had been mistaken then they would have to consider seriously if there was any reasonable doubt against the accused man.

The jury was absent for only fifty minutes before finding the prisoner guilty. Asked by the clerk of the court if he had anything to say why sentence of death should not be passed upon him, Paul held up his left hand, in which he held a rosary, and replied, 'I am not guilty, my lord.' Mr Justice Asquith pronounced sentence of death. Despite his protestations of innocence, Sidney Paul decided not to appeal against his death sentence, and the date of the execution was set for 20 December at Pentonville Prison, but less than a week before it was announced that the Home Secretary had recommended a reprieve.

There can be little doubt that Sidney Paul, at the end of his tether both financially and emotionally, murdered his wife. The fires may well have been arson, the earlier burglary fictitious, either for an insurance fraud or to add verisimilitude to his later claims. Sidney's cut wrist in September could have been a failed suicide attempt.

Comparing the supposedly conflicting evidence of the Coopers reveals that there really was no conflict at all. They had looked out of the window at slightly different moments and seen slightly different stages of the tragedy. Mrs Cooper's view of a person with their hands on Sidney's shoulders was interpreted by the defence as suggesting the presence of a third person, an intruder, but this is not necessarily the case. Both Coopers saw a stooping person in dark clothes. Mrs Cooper's stooping person could not be identified as male or female. Mr Cooper's was undoubtedly a woman and must have been Claire Paul. It seems reasonable that Mrs Cooper's stooping person was also Claire Paul, shortly after being attacked, leaning on her husband, possibly pleading for mercy. A few moments later, while she lay on the ground, Sidney administered the final fatal injuries.

Sidney Paul served his sentence at Camp Hill Prison, Isle of Wight. A report written in 1942 stated that he was in fair health and continued to maintain his innocence. While well-behaved and hard-working, he was not well liked. The chaplain described him as '... most untrustworthy, cunning and criminally disposed ...' while the governor found him '... almost without humour, calculating, hard and selfish ...' The report concluded that 'an unduly favourable view' had been taken when he was reprieved. In January 1946, however, Paul petitioned the Home Secretary for release, saying, 'I am now an old man [he was 53] and am filled with contrition on account of my crime.' He was released on license on 15 November.

# 10

# A BIT OF A FIX

## *Greenford, 1941*

In December 1940 Mrs Lillian Bound came to live at the upper flat, No. 9A Goring Way, Greenford, which she shared with her married daughter Heather Thomas and son-in-law Lewis. The ground floor flat, No. 9, was occupied by a young couple and a child. Lionel Watson was 30 years old. He had been working as a bakelite moulder at the Hoover Factory in Perivale off Western Avenue since January 1940, and had met attractive fair-haired Phyllis Crocker when she started work at the factory the following August. Twenty-six-year-old Phyllis was the daughter of a law clerk, the late Harry Crocker, and his wife Alice. Phyllis had a daughter, Eileen, born in November 1939, the result of a liaison with a man she had later found was married. When Phyllis joined Hoover she was living at the Goring Way flat with her mother and Eileen, but in September her mother, nervous of air raids, had gone to stay with a sister in Scotland. Soon afterwards, Lionel Watson moved in with Phyllis.

Watson was open about the fact that he was a married man, although separated from his wife, and with four children, three of whom had been evacuated from London and were living with a Mrs Sydenham in Weston-super-Mare. Phyllis even went with Lionel to visit the children. In October 1940 Phyllis's mother returned to live at Goring Way, but still tormented by nerves she threw herself in the river at Twickenham. She was rescued and removed to hospital, where she died on 2 November. Alice Crocker left her daughter the sum of £200, which Phyllis paid into in a Post Office account. In addition to this modest investment she owned a share certificate.

Lillian Bound and Phyllis soon became good friends and saw each other several times a day. Sometimes they communicated by knocking on the floor, and they often had early morning tea together in Phyllis's kitchenette. On 22 December, Phyllis went into hospital, returning home on 4 January. Mrs Bound did not know it at the time, but Phyllis had suffered a septic abortion, the termination of a pregnancy due to infection of the uterus. There was no reason to suppose that this was anything other than spontaneous. Despite the loss of both her mother and unborn child

*Goring Way, Greenford.*

within two months of each other, the young woman seemed to be in good health and spirits, indeed everyone who spoke of Phyllis commented on the fact that she had a sunny and cheerful disposition. It seemed that she had a smile for everyone. Mrs Bound described Phyllis as 'a very bright girl, real good company.' Phyllis and Lionel appeared to be happy together and he helped her in the house and with her daughter when she was feeling unwell. Neighbours who were unaware that they were not husband and wife referred to them as 'the perfect married couple'. The occasional mild squabbles were about money, as Lionel sometimes only worked a part week at Hoovers.

The only person who disapproved of the relationship between Phyllis and Lionel was Lionel's mother Ellen. She had told Phyllis openly that she was against any association between her and Lionel and that it was wrong for a single girl to have an illegitimate child. Ellen had once had a row with Phyllis on the doorstep, accusing her of keeping Lionel away from his wife and children. 'What sort of woman do you call yourself?' she said, then turned and walked away.

On the 18 January 1941, Phyllis had good reason to be more than usually cheerful. Lionel had told her that his solicitor had called to say that his wife had finally granted him the divorce he had asked for, and on that day, Lionel Watson and Phyllis Crocker were married. Phyllis asked for the tenancy of the flat to be transferred to the name of her new husband, but something about Lionel caused the estate manager to refuse to carry this out. The manager later commented, 'Not being impressed with Mr Watson, this was not done.' Unfortunately he did not elaborate.

In May Phyllis told Mrs Bound that she suspected that she was pregnant again as she was suffering from bouts of morning sickness. She did not seem unhappy at the prospect. 'She said she did not mind if she was pregnant or not,' said Lillian Bound, later. Although Phyllis went to her doctor to get medication for the sickness, she did not mention to him that she thought she might be pregnant. Dr Stewart saw Phyllis a number of times regarding the occasional vomiting, and prescribed a gastric sedative. The last time he saw her was on 5 May, when she had seemed very much better.

On 18 May, Phyllis visited a friend, Ruby Tattershall, and appeared to be well and happy. On the following day Phyllis showed Lillian some new clothes she had bought for herself and Eileen from a clothing club into which she paid a shilling a week. She seemed very pleased with her purchases. The next morning, at about 10.30, Mrs Bound saw Phyllis hanging out some washing on the clothes line and said 'Hello'. 'She seemed quite jolly,' Mrs Bound said later.

Lillian did not see Phyllis or Eileen at all the next day. When the baker's roundsman delivered bread at 2.30 that afternoon Lionel Watson answered the door and said he didn't want any more bread after that day. The same evening Lionel took Mrs Bound a bottle of milk, something he occasionally did when he had one spare. She paid for the milk, and asked him where Phyllis was. He said that she had gone away to Scotland very early in the morning because she had received a letter from her aunt enclosing money for her fare. 'You were very quiet last night,' said Mrs Bound. Lionel explained that they had gone to bed early because of the long journey in the morning. She noticed that he was very agitated; his face was pale and his hands and head were shaking.

On 22 May Mrs Bound heard the sound of a great deal of scrubbing and sweeping in the flat below, and there was a strong smell of pine disinfectant.

On the 23rd she saw Lionel in the garden and asked if he had heard from Phyllis yet. When he said he had, she asked for Phyllis's address so she could write. Lionel felt in his pockets and said he had left the letter 'at home'. She gathered from that statement that he was no longer living at the flat. He promised he would bring her the address, but the next time she saw him he said, 'I might as well tell you that Phyllis did not wish to correspond with anyone round here. In fact she would like to get away from the flat.' Mrs Bound felt very hurt at this and did not ask after Phyllis again. Lionel did, however, ask if she could lend him a spade.

On 26 May Mrs Bound saw Watson digging in the back garden near the coal house. There had been a row of flagstones by the side of the coal house forming a path and he had lifted them and was digging underneath. She asked if he was 'digging for victory' and he said he was burying some rubbish. The hole, when finished, was over 6ft in length and about 2ft wide and 2ft deep. The next day she saw that he had finished his work and the flagstones were back in place.

Although the downstairs flat was unoccupied, Mrs Bound heard people there from time to time over the next few weeks. There had been an unusually cool spring that year and the first ten days of June were miserably cold and wet. All the same, Mrs Bound began to notice an unpleasant smell in the garden coming from under the flagstones. After 10 June, the rain stopped, the sun appeared and temperatures began to climb. By the 15th it was a pleasant 70 degrees Fahrenheit, but the weather continued to grow steadily warmer. The 22 June 1941 was one of the hottest June days on record, thermometers recording over 90 degrees. The smell in the garden grew worse and Mrs Bound mentioned it to her neighbour, Mrs Burgess.

On 27 June Lionel was back, watering the garden, and she noticed that the water he used looked white and thick, and smelled strongly of pine disinfectant.

On 30 June Mrs Bound and Mrs Burgess decided to investigate. They entered the downstairs flat and had a look around, but noticed nothing unusual. They then went into the garden and took up one of the flagstones, revealing the top layer of earth and some white powder. The ground all around had been heavily disinfected. Mrs Bound touched something that lay underneath the powder and there was a hiss of escaping gas. The stench was so overpowering that she had to move away. The women told Mr Burgess of what they had found, and he went to investigate further. Pulling up a flagstone, he was greeted by an appalling smell. He dropped the flag-stone back in place and they all agreed to go to the police station and report what they had found. At that point, all they had to describe was a rubbish nuisance, but when they returned Mr Burgess couldn't resist having another look. This time he removed some earth. He soon returned to the police saying that he thought he had found human flesh.

Two CID officers arrived, removed the slabs and began carefully clearing away the earth beneath, revealing the shape of a human hand lying as if folded across the chest. They removed more earth and saw the outline of a human body. Messages were sent summoning Inspectors Smith and Deighton, who arrived the same evening, and digging continued through the hours of darkness, with only the sound of spades and the occasional flash of a torch to disturb the neighbours.

As the work continued, the shape emerged of a young woman lying fully stretched out on her back. She was wearing only a cellular vest and a lace petticoat. The body was wrapped in two pieces of sheeting and sprinkled with garden lime. Nestled by the woman's left leg was the body of a child wrapped in a cotton blanket. Both bodies were heavily decomposed and had obviously been there for some weeks. The bodies were later identified by Mrs Bound as Phyllis and Eileen.

Inspector Smith searched the flat for anything suspicious and found a file and hacksaw blade, which had grains of white powder clinging to them.

At 6.55 a.m. on 1 July, Deighton and Smith went to the Hoover factory, where they awaited the arrival of Lionel Watson. Intercepting him at the factory entrance Deighton said, 'We are police officers. I am making enquiries in respect of your wife and child.' Watson said, 'I know. Don't show me up here. There is no need to hold me. I found them dead. Let's go in here.' They went into the timekeeper's lodge.

Deighton cautioned Watson and said that they had found the bodies and would take him to Greenford police station. In Watson's first statement to the police he began by referring to Phyllis as his wife, but eventually he admitted that he had lied to her about the divorce and had married her bigamously. He said he had married Phyllis 'to make her happy'. This theme in Watson's statements, whereby he explained his actions by saying that he had selflessly done things for others, was to repeat itself.

Phyllis, he claimed, had not wanted another pregnancy because of the hard time she had had giving birth to Eileen, and she had used a syringe for contraception. In March she had told him that she was pregnant again and was very upset. In April she had suffered from quinsy and tonsillitis and had been 'a bit run down'. He said that Phyllis had taken a number of substances to procure an abortion including gin and Epsom salts, and had been ill in bed for two days because of this.

Tuesday 20 May had been his day off work, and Phyllis had not been feeling well and had gone to bed. She was worried because she had had a letter from Eileen's father about the 10s a week child support he was supposed to have been paying her and which had not been paid for some time. She said he was afraid of going to prison because of this. Watson told the police that he had gone out to the cinema at 5.30 p.m. Appreciating that this might have sounded selfish, he explained that he hadn't wanted to go out, he had wanted to stay with Phyllis but she had pressed him to go out and he had done so to please her.

According to Watson, he had returned home at about ten and found Phyllis lying on the floor outside the bathroom door. She had been sick. He patted her face as he thought she had fainted or had a fit, but realised that she was dead. He went to the baby's room and found her dead.

'I was very upset,' he said. 'I was in a bit of a fix, because I had bigamously married her. That occurred to me at the time. I could not call a doctor by reason of that because it would all come out that I had bigamously married her and I thought of my children and my people and my job.'

Watson said that he had initially thought of hiding the bodies in a trunk but realised on second thoughts that they would smell too much and decided to bury them. He put the bodies in the hole under cover of darkness and sprinkled them with garden lime. He then returned the borrowed spade to Mrs Bound and went back to live with his mother.

On 1 July Sir Bernard Spilsbury carried out the post-mortem at Hayes mortuary. At first glance there appeared to be no obvious cause of death, since both bodies were intact without any external marks of violence. Phyllis was in good health, and she was three months pregnant. It was a normal pregnancy and there was no indication that she had done anything to abort the foetus. The stomachs of both bodies contained some reddish material and the interior membranes showed signs of irritant poisoning. The stomachs and their contents with the liver and kidneys were removed and taken to Home Office analyst Dr Gerald Roche Lynch, who reported that the cause of death was poisoning with sodium cyanide.

Cyanide, used in a number of industrial processes, was usually stored as hard white lumps of material. If reduced to a fine powder, however, it could be sprinkled

*Sir Bernard Spilsbury.*

on food where it would have very little taste. The victim could eat it without detecting that anything was wrong and unconsciousness and death would follow rapidly. Roche Lynch also found traces of cyanide on the file and hacksaw, and thought that this was the method used to powder the material.

When Watson's fellow workers at the Hoover factory were questioned, it emerged that he had been showing a recent interest in poisons and cyanide in particular, which was used in the case-hardening process and was stored at the factory in steel drums.

Frederick Heath was a bakelite moulder who worked with Watson. He had seen Watson in the case-hardening department with a white powder, which he had said was poisonous and could be used for killing insects in the garden.

Alfred Halls also worked there and said he had seen Watson with a lump of something he said was caustic soda which he wanted to use to clean the bath.

Another fellow worker, Ernest Bradshaw, said that he and Watson had sometimes discussed 'home matters', and Watson knew that Bradshaw's wife suffered from a heart condition. One day at the end of April or beginning of May Watson had asked Bradshaw if he could bring him some of 'his wife's poison tablets'. 'Whatever for?' asked Bradshaw in astonishment. Watson replied that he had a dog to kill. Bradshaw told him that the tablets were no good for that, they were only sleeping tablets.

Leonard Honey told the police that on 17 May Watson had tried to sell him a share certificate, saying he wanted to raise some money. Honey told Watson he didn't want it.

Joan Filby was 17½ and had worked at Hoover since September 1940. From March 1941 she had known Watson only to say 'hello' in passing, but he had obviously had his eye on the attractive redhead. On 21 May, which was most probably

*Hoover Building.*

two days after Phyllis and Eileen's deaths, Lionel Watson slipped a note to Joan asking her to go out with him. At first she took no notice, because she already had a boyfriend. At the start of June he again asked her out, and eventually she agreed. Their first date was on 4 June. They had several dates, Lionel taking Joan dancing, on a river trip and to the cinema. He told her he was divorced and living with his mother and made her presents of jewellery.

On 15 June he took her to the flat at Goring Way and offered her some shoes and a coat he said had belonged to his first wife. She didn't take them. He also showed her some hats, frocks and two fur coats and said she could have them, but she refused those too. According to Joan he never took any liberties with her apart from a kiss and cuddle. It was getting late and she went home. Next morning he brought a dress and some shoes to the factory and gave them to her. Other gifts he made to Joan were a small bottle of scent, a photograph of himself and a page of margarine coupons.

Well before the finding of the bodies, Joan had ended the relationship, saying that she couldn't see him any more as she already had a 'young man'.

On the day before he was arrested he wrote her a note:

I expect you wonder why I picked you out of all the girls there is. Well, because I took to you as soon as I saw you. You are a lot different to some of them, and I was beginning to love you, which I still do, even if you have a boyfriend. Perhaps there is room for me somewhere …

She didn't reply as she had already decided that she wanted nothing more to do with him.

Joan wasn't the only person to receive gifts. Mrs Eileen Rose Ross had known Watson for many years and knew about his relationship with Phyllis. She had last seen Lionel on 24 June when he said that Phyllis had gone to an aunt in Scotland who had lots of money and was going to furnish her out with a house. He gave Mrs Ross a bracelet and a serviette ring which had an E engraved on it. The latter may well have been a christening gift to baby Eileen. Mrs Ross later gave them to the police.

Despite Mrs Watson's adamant statement that her son would never intentionally hurt anyone, his estranged wife, Alice, had another tale to tell. The marriage, said Alice, had never been satisfactory as Lionel used to go around with another girl. She had obtained a separation on the grounds of cruelty. He had once punched her in the face and as a result she had lost the sight in one eye.

Police enquiries soon revealed that Watson had a criminal record. There were four offences of petty theft for which he had been bound over, and on 6 September 1938 he had been convicted for office breaking, stealing cash and postal orders and forging a postal order. Sentenced to eighteen months hard labour, he had come out of prison in December 1939 to find that his wife had left him for another man.

After Phyllis's death Lionel had written to the Post Office forging Phyllis's signature to try and withdraw the money from her account. The Post Office had sent back the form saying they were not satisfied with the signature and he had abandoned the attempt.

On 2 July Watson asked to see Inspector Deighton, saying that there were some things he wanted to explain. He was cautioned and said that after he had found Phyllis dead he took some of her jewellery to the pawnbrokers. He explained that he had done this because it had been Phyllis's wish not to be buried with jewellery on. Deighton went to the pawnbrokers and took possession of the jewellery, which consisted of two rings, a pendant and a bracelet.

Ruby Tattershall later identified some face powder, a compact, jewellery, gloves, shoes and a dress in the possession of Joan Filby as the property of Phyllis. She also identified as her friend's the jewellery found at the pawnbrokers.

Watson was formally charged with the murder of Phyllis and Eileen Crocker, which he denied, saying he had found them dead. He said that Phyllis had asked him to give away her clothes as they were too small for her, and he needed the money from the Post Office to pay off the hire purchase on the furniture.

Lionel Watson was certified sane and fit to plead by Dr Grierson of Brixton Prison, and the trial opened at the Central Criminal Court, Old Bailey on Monday, 15 September 1941. The prisoner pleaded not guilty.

The prosecutors were Mr G.B. McClure and Mr Christmas Humphreys, with Mr J.P. Valetta and Mr Durand appearing for the defence.

Mrs Bound testified as to Phyllis's good health and spirits during the month of May, describing her as 'cheerful and happy' when she had last seen her. The young woman had never suggested she wanted to abort the baby and had never appeared

*Christmas Humphreys.*

to be depressed. Phyllis did not own a dog, but Mrs Bound's son-in-law had one. Watson had liked the dog and no one had ever suggested poisoning it.

Mrs Burgess said that Phyllis was 'always jolly and bright' and in May she had been planning a holiday. Phyllis was 'never depressed so as to do herself or her child an injury', and unlike her mother was not especially nervous of air raids.

Phyllis's ration book showed that she had had no intention of leaving Greenford, as no application had been made for the transference of her rations to another district.

Dr T.W. Stewart said he had no reason to suppose that Phyllis had taken anything to abort the pregnancy which ended in December 1940, and had never known her to take any medication apart from that which he had prescribed.

Roche Lynch testified that he was surprised that he had been able to find traces of cyanide in the remains. The bodies had been buried for some six to seven weeks before he tested the samples, and in many recorded cases of death from cyanide it had disappeared entirely from the body in similar or shorter periods of time. The fact that it was still present convinced him that a considerable amount had been taken, and that death was due to cyanide poisoning.

The case for the defence was that Phyllis had committed suicide because she was pregnant. Her mother's suicide attempt and subsequent death in a mental home was a strong point in favour of this argument, and it was also revealed that Phyllis's father, who had been taken to hospital after being knocked down by a car, had subsequently died in a mental institution.

Lionel Watson gave evidence in his own defence. He said that Phyllis had asked him to marry her when he was divorced, and he had said he would, but his wife would not give him a divorce so he had married Phyllis bigamously. She had been very ill after her last visit to Ruby Tattershall on 18 May, and on the following day Phyllis had complained of a headache and taken some aspirin. When he got home from the cinema he had found her lying 'head outward from the bathroom' and the baby dead. 'I picked up Phyllis's hand and stroked it,' he said. 'I remembered she had a wish never to have jewellery on her, so I took the rings off her fingers and put them in my pocket.' The next morning he had thrown them away.

Watson claimed that he had asked about poisons at the factory because he knew that Mrs Bound's son-in-law wanted to put the dog to sleep. He knew about cyanide but did not use it in the course of his work. He admitted that had taken some home but this was only to kill insects in the garden and for cleaning purposes. He had shown the lump of white material to Phyllis and told her not to touch it as it was poison. He had then used the hacksaw and file to break it up, and all of the powder had been used to clean the lavatory. Watson said he thought Phyllis must have taken a piece of the cyanide before he had filed it to powder, and hidden it intending to use it. He denied that he had tried to sell Phyllis's share certificate, claiming that Phyllis had given it to him to see if he could borrow on it.

Admitting that he had dated Joan Filby, Watson told the court, 'I did it for companionship. I was very upset. I was depressed after losing Phyllis like that.'

Watson's explanation for the deaths of Phyllis and Eileen was that Phyllis had murdered her own child and then committed suicide. He then made one of his few truthful statements: '... it was to save my own skin that I buried the bodies.'

Mr Christmas Humphreys addressed the jury. 'You cannot ignore in the background of this case those old factors in criminal cases – women and money. Watch the mind of the man as it moves from woman to woman ...' Holding up a tiny test tube of cyanide to the jury he said, 'he comes away with a fistful, when that much means death!'

Mr Valetta for the defence tried to convince the jury that Phyllis was obsessed with not wanting to bear another child. He pointed out that her father and mother had both died in mental institutions and suggested that she might have killed Eileen and taken her own life on an impulse.

While the judge was summing up a woman juror was taken ill and was allowed to leave the court. On her return the judge passed her a small bottle of smelling salts and she resumed her seat.

The jury was absent for only twenty minutes before finding Watson guilty. The prisoner stood unmoved as Mr Justice Cassells donned the black cap. 'Upon overwhelming evidence the jury have found you guilty of murder,' he said. 'You planned to poison Phyllis Crocker, and you did so.' He then pronounced sentence of death. As Watson left the dock he glanced at his father, who was sitting only a few feet away.

*Mr Justice Cassels.*

Watson felt that Ruby Tattershall had more to say about Phyllis's state of mind at her last visit on 18 May, and should have given evidence about this at the trial. He wrote to Ruby from Pentonville Prison on 1 October imploring her to reveal what she knew. She had nothing further to impart.

Watson's appeal was heard on 17 October and Mr Valetta appeared on his behalf, with Mr McClure representing the Crown. The grounds of the appeal were that the judge in his summing up had not dealt adequately with the evidence relating to the defence's claim that Phyllis had administered poison to her infant daughter and committed suicide.

The Lord Chief Justice, Viscount Caldecote, said that there was a great body of evidence connecting Watson with the deaths which was 'sufficient to prove to the hilt the charge made against him if the jury believed it.' He found no grounds for Mr Valetta's criticism. The appeal was dismissed.

Watson petitioned for mercy on 1 November. He mentioned 'two new vital witnesses to come forward with great importance with this case'. Those witnesses were his mother and the lady who cared for his children, Mrs Sydenham. Mrs Watson had stated that Phyllis had told her that she had felt so disgraced and 'shown up' when she had the first child that if she thought she was going to have another she would do away with herself. Mrs Sydenham had later told the Watsons that Phyllis had made a similar statement on one of her visits to Weston-super-Mare. Watson's father, Oscar Rupert Watson, wrote to the Home Secretary, Herbert Morrison, on 7 November, pointing out that this evidence had never been brought for the

*Pentonville Prison.*

defence at the trial. Whether or not Phyllis really had made those statements was never determined, although even if she had done, it could have been countered by the argument that at the time of her death Phyllis had believed herself to be a married woman.

On 11 November it was confirmed that there were no grounds for granting a respite.

In his letters to his friends and relatives Watson maintained right up to the end that Phyllis had committed suicide. On the eve of execution he wrote to his parents; 'do not look on Phyllis for the cause of my downfall, as she did not know it was going to lead to this as I expected she thought she was doing the right thing for me to leave me free ...' He makes no suggestion as to why Phyllis might have wanted to leave him free, but then it was in character for Watson to transfer all the intentions and motivations from himself to the woman he had killed. Even though he continued the fiction of her suicide, the letters show the calm acceptance of his fate often seen in the last words of those who have come to terms with their guilt.

On Wednesday, 12 November 1941, Watson was hanged at Pentonville.

# BIBLIOGRAPHY

## GENERAL SOURCES

Genealogy data accessed www.ancestry.com
International Genealogical Index accessed www.familyseach.org
Trials accessed www.oldbaileyonline.org
Contemporary newspapers

## SPECIFIC SOURCES

### 1. MURDER ON THE HEATH
London Metropolitan Archives ACC/1126/004
Newgate calendar accessed http://www.exclassics.com/newgate/ng481.htm
James Harmer, *Murder of Mr. Steele. Documents and observations tending to shew a probability of the innocence of J. Holloway and O. Haggerty, who were executed ... as the murderers of the above gentleman* (London, 1807)

### 2. THE BEADLE OF ENFIELD
P. Egan, *Boxiana* (4 vols London, Sherwood, Neely and Jones, 1818), vol. 2 pp. 198–211

### 3. MURDER IN MAD BESS WOOD
National Archives
PRO HO 64/7

### 4. IN THE HEAT OF THE MOMENT
Sylvanus Urban (ed.), *The Gentleman's Magazine* (London, William Pickering, John Bowyer Nichols and Son) 1800 vol. 70 July–December p. 792 and 1840 vol. 168 January–June, p. 667
National Archives
PRO TS 11/897/3062
PRO PROB 11/2169
PRO C 101/3800

### 5. THE WINE SHOP MURDER
National Archives
PRO CRIM 1/179/3

## 6. BLAMING A WOMAN

National Archives
PRO HO 144/1631/406003/1
PCOM 8/65/1
PRO MEPO 3/269
HO 144/1631/406003
PRO CRIM 1/185/3
PRO PCOM 8/65

## 7. THE RUBBISH DUMP MURDER

D.G. Browne, and E.V. Tullett, *Bernard Spilsbury, His Life and Cases* (London, George G. Harrap
 & Co., 1951)
National Archives
CRIM 1/560
MEPO 3/865
HO 144/15018

## 8. THE WIDOW OF TWICKENHAM

National Archives
MEPO 3/1712

## 9. THE MAN WITH A SCAR

National Archives
PRO MEPO 1/1735
PRO MEPO 3/1735
PRO DPP 1/580
PRO DPP 2/580
PRO CRIM 1/585
PRO HO 144/22664
PRO HO 144/22665
PRO CRIM 1/1050

## 10. A BIT OF A FIX

National Archives
PRO HO 144/21533
PRO CRIM 1/1337
PRO MEPO 3/2186
PRO PCOM 9/826

# INDEX

Other titles published by The History Press

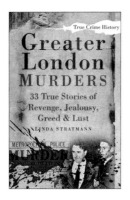

## Greater London Murders
### 33 True Stories of Revenge, Jealousy, Greed & Lust
LINDA STRATMANN

Throughout its history the great urban sprawl of Greater London has been home to some of the most shocking murders in England. Contained within the pages of this book are the stories behind these heinous crimes. They include George Chapman, who was hanged in 1903 for poisoning three women, and whom is widely suspected of having been the notorious serial killer Jack the Ripper; and Donald Hume, who was found not guilty of the murder of wealthy businessman Stanley Setty in 1949, but later confessed to killing him, chopping up his body and disposing of it by aeroplane. Linda Stratmann has also unearthed astounding new information that sheds a whole new light on the infamous Craig and Bentley case.

978 0 7524 5124 4

## Kent Murders
LINDA STRATMANN

Contained within the pages of this book are the stories behind some of the most notorious murders in Kent's history. Among the gruesome cases featured here area the doctor who was poisoned with morphine in Faversham; the couple who were brutally battered to death in their beds in Chislehurst; and the strange death of a young German man whose body was discovered with one hand missing on Ramsgate beach.

978 0 7509 4811 1

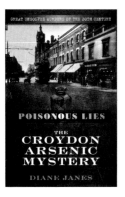

## Poisonous Lies
### The Croydon Arsenic Mystery
DIANE JANES

In suburban Croydon over a period of ten months during 1928–9, three members of the same family died suddenly. A complex police investigation followed, but no charges were ever brought and the mystery remains officially unsolved. In the eighty years which followed, the finger of suspicion has been pointed at one member of the family after another: now, using the original police files and other contemporary documents, Diane Janes meticulously reconstructs these astonishing events and offers a new solution to an old murder mystery.

978 0 7524 5337 8

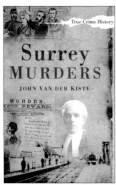

## Surrey Murders
JOHN VAN DER KISTE

*Surrey Murders* is an examination of some of the county's most notorious and shocking cases. They include the 'Wigwam Girl', Joan Wolfe, who lived in a tent built by a Cree Indian Soldier before being brutally slaughtered; the infamous stabbing of Frederick Gold by 'the Serpent', Percy Lefroy Mapleton; the poisoning of the entire Beck family with a bottle of oatmeal stout, laced with cyanide; and the sailor butchered at the Devil's Punch Bowl, later immortalised in Charles Dickens' *Nicholas Nickleby*.

978 0 7509 5130 2

Visit our website and discover thousands of other History Press books.

# www.thehistorypress.co.uk

The History Press